How Long Did it Take?

WENDY MURPHY

Cover painting: Wendy Murphy

FOR CERI AND MIHANGEL JONES

With special thanks to Mihangel and Ceri Jones for all their words of wisdom, help, enthusiasm and support, throughout the production of this book and to Lavinia and Robin Range for their encouragement and all the lovely meals. Also, thank you to my family and friends that spurred me on.

'Art' with a capital 'A' is a monumental word, under which umbrella there are many facets; encompassing Music, Performance art, Literature, Fine art, Photography, Design, - each one of these with their own sub-cultures of diversity.

I have focused on the area of Art that I am most familiar with, so any reference to 'Artists' refers mainly to my own experience as a painter, and that of various people that I have met, working in the same field, rather than that of artists working in other genres.

Part One is the starter, providing a brief background and an introduction to the stage in my life when I was in my late twenties, having decided to leave my 'sensible life' in order to pursue a more unstable, but creative path.

Part Two is the main course. Emerging into the real world again after five years of study, this is really where my life as a painter begins…….

I apologise in advance to all the people I will upset.

PART ONE

FROM RICHES TO RAGS

Wendy Murphy

When I was in my late twenties I lost all my senses and decided to make the transition from being a 'normal person' (or a civilian), in order to join the ranks of weirdos and become an artist; giving up a well-paid job, complete with holidays, a house, regular subscriptions to Clarin's and a husband, not to mention the security of knowing when the next pay cheque would arrive, for a life of hardship, struggle and more often than not anguish.

The trigger for this mad change of direction was the fault of my eight-year old nephew, or rather his set of dubious quality paints that he had left at my house whilst visiting.

I was off work, no doubt swinging the lead, (anything for a day off) and feeling a bit bored, thought I'd try my hand at a spot of dabbling with the abandoned paints. By the end of the afternoon I had produced three amazing little pictures, (amazingly awful that is), that I had copied from photographs in a magazine, one of which my sister I am embarrassed to say still has on her living room wall. In fact one of her favourite laments, over thirty years later, is still "I don't know why you can't do more little scenes like this one, you know, things people would like". I have tried explaining that I've moved on and spent years developing as a painter in order not to produce such tat, but alas she is immovable.

I believe the illness at this time that had made me

temporarily unfit for work, may have not only rendered me slightly delirious but also delusional, because I was convinced that the 'sunset at sea', the 'cottage garden' complete with old-fashioned girl in a white pinny and the 'labrador puppies in a basket' that finished up looking more like scampi and chips, were in fact good. No, not just good, I could see that they had the equivalent of whatever the X-factor was in those days. I realised that my true vocation had merely been temporarily misplaced and was in fact just round the corner.

When my husband at the time (notice where he came on the list of assets) arrived home from work in the evening, I had really built up to a crescendo and waving my mini masterpieces in his face, I announced dramatically that I was going to become an artist. Whereupon he looked at me wearily and said "don't be so bloody daft"......

*   *   *

You may be forgiven for thinking that my entry into the world of art was more to do with 'right I'll show the bastard' but actually you would be wrong. Dramatic and unlikely though it may sound, I did genuinely have a bit of a revelation on that day and I was convinced that ART was what I needed to be doing.

As a child I hadn't exactly been considered to be an 'all rounder'. In fact I don't think I was even spherical. For a start I wasn't a team player, but was in fact allergic to all sporting activities. I knew this because of all the sick notes that my mother had procured over the years. In fact I think it likely that I inherited much of my creative imagination from my mother; "please excuse Wendy from PE today as she has a cold/stomach ache / diarrhoea / verrucas / measles / leprosy / fear of moving".....on and on...... by the time she had exhausted the potential in the 'Family Medical Practitioner' book she kept by her side, she would begin again with the common cold. I have to say she showed an impressive ability to embellish even the most mundane complaints. There are only so many believable ways you can suggest that someone be excused from taking part in an activity that they find excruciatingly awful, but she did her best and we felt that 'allergy' was as good a word as any to collectively describe all those nasty symptoms that I experienced as a little girl. I believe I did actually have a few of the complaints at odd times.

I am not being strictly honest when I say that I was crap at games because there was one exception to my physical ineptitude .... I could climb ropes.

One of the most hated 'games' (I seriously question this choice of word) that we were forced to participate in, was that of 'Pirates', whereby all the most terrifying objects of torture in the school hall, such as the box, the horse and the climbing frame were procured. Even the mats held their own terror, in the shape of us having to perform forward rolls (in my case not achieved until the age of eleven and three-quarters), despite spending years practicing on my bed at home. When other girls were starting to think about make-up and sanitary towels, there I was straining the springs. As I grew, my mother begged me to stop, fearing she would have to fork out for a new bed.

My ecstasy in finally achieving this goal was short-lived, because the really tragic thing is that whilst I'd been determinedly hurling myself along the mattress, I had failed to notice that this childish activity had been usurped by a new terror ..... netball, where I would be screeched at by Mrs Brock to "run towards the ball Wendy, not away from it".

I have gone through my adult life feeling cheated that my achievement with the roll has never been recognised. I just haven't found there has been much call for that sort of thing. The closest I've come to the type of mat that doesn't go in front of the fire since schooldays, was when I once attended a yoga class, but as a middle-aged woman, I could hardly start showing-off and rolling around, when everyone else was tying themselves in knots, could I?

Anyway, the rules of the 'pirate' ordeal were such that if your feet at any time touched the floor it meant that you had gone overboard and were out of the game. Thinking I could outwit Mrs B, by simply standing on the floor, it didn't take her long to scream at me to get off my sea of safety and join in.

I think my prowess at shinning up ropes was born out of desperation to get as far away from the activities below as possible. I became quite adept at it and spent many a happy lesson hanging on for grim death up in the rafters like a little ginger monkey until the game was finished, and having decided I was a lost cause, Mrs Brock would look a little sad and say "alright Wendy you can come down now".

The fact is, despite the fact that I didn't have a lazy eye, wear national health glasses or possess an anorak (although I was ginger), I was to all intents and purposes a misfit, a nerd. I was that sad child that had to be placed by the teacher in the team otherwise chosen by one of the kids with the Colgate ring of confidence, as no self-respecting pupil would want me on their side.

I did quite enjoy geography until the teacher realized that I couldn't differentiate between Africa and Italy, but derived great pleasure from drawing and colouring in the maps; the areas within them could have been slices of pizza for all I knew.

I had particularly enjoyed these lessons, before I was rumbled, as the view from the geography room window overlooked the adjacent boys' school playing fields and on occasions we girls would get a tantalizing glimpse of muddy knees.

The only subjects aside from art that I was quite good at, were English (I believe I learnt a lot about the art of storytelling from my mother), and surprisingly biology, although this may have been triggered by the muddy knees.

I think the least said about my ability in Maths the better, except to say that I truly believe that the side of my brain that deals with all that stuff was gobbled up at birth by the artistic side.

Anyway, where all this is leading, the point I am coming to, is that the general consensus regarding my formative years was "Oh well never mind, she's quite artistic", which if we're being honest here, meant 'she's not like the rest of us, she's a bit odd'.

My parents were quite prepared to turn a blind eye to my 'individuality', presumably in the hope that I would grow out of it. So it was unfortunate really, that any seed of talent that I may have possessed at that time, was not planted in fertile soil, because my art teacher at the dubious comprehensive that I attended, a Miss Jones, had a different agenda to the one she was being paid for, and was not I imagine even aware of my existence, let alone any artistic skills I may have possessed.

She would plonk a few pots and pans down in the middle of a table, I believe this was considered to be a 'still life' and tell us to "Get on with it girls", before disappearing into the store room with Mr Baxter the maths teacher, whilst the more forward girls would discuss over the pots and pans, the thrilling prospect of what might be going on behind that closed door. To twelve year old girls (remember this was still the 60's), the shocking notion that they might be 'having it off' added an air of glamour to our otherwise dreary class. Madam Jones and Mr B would reappear, five minutes apart, looking flushed and disheveled at the end of the lesson, when we would be told "all right girls you can clear up now".

I don't ever remember receiving any comments on the fruits of our labour and have harboured a dislike for still-life ever since. I did however learn a valuable lesson from Miss Jones in the art of becoming a con-artist.

*   *   *

Having grown up on a huge rambling council estate, I had left school aged fifteen (you could in those days), and coming from the sort of background where further education meant hanging around after school at the bus stop in the hope of catching a glimpse of David Rickman, I didn't have a clue as to how to go about forging ahead with planning my new intended career.

I had been too busy growing up and trying to jump

onto the moving train that had a reserved seat with my name already on it, to be aware that there could be any other mode of travel I might consider taking on the journey of my life.

It was real 'Educating Rita' stuff. For several years, I managed to convince my family, and myself, that I had indeed grown out of all that sensitive artistic stuff – for heavens sake, what good would an ability to draw ever do me. But the creative seed had not quite been buried and had quietly begun to worm it's way to the surface.

I was at the time of my little artistic forage, working as a typesetter in London. As I mentioned, I had a house, a husband (albeit one with a roving eye) and a three hour a day commute from Kent to London, and although my job was well-paid, I knew I was in the wrong life. If I am honest I had been feeling increasingly dissatisfied and unfulfilled in my working life for a while so I was ready for adventure.

*   *   *

The thirteen years I spent working as a typesetter seemed to involve a great deal of time travelling up to London, travelling home from London, travelling up to London, travelling home from London, travelling up to London, travelling home from London on and on and on

…. I was on a very non-creative treadmill, still a bit of the jigsaw that didn't quite fit, only this time trying to force myself into office world instead of school.

On reflection, the most interesting time then was probably spent on the train, it's a pity really that there had to be the bit in between to spoil it. This time spent in limbo was great in some ways and could be used as productively or not as I chose. I might read or just day-dream through the window, or I could join the dribbling rubber necked lollers in sleep (patterned ties are always best). Even the nose pickers and pervs, who would rub their leg against the side of any unlucky female that happened to be sitting alongside them, had their rightful place in the carriage.

During one of the commuting years I used my time very admirably by studying for three O'levels by way of correspondence course with 'The Rapid Results' college, in order to prove to myself that I was capable of passing an exam. Pity really that all this was going on before I'd had the 'calling' so I didn't think to carry a sketchbook around with me at this time.

As regulars of the 'commuter club', we each had our own position on the train; in my case in the right-hand corner, by the window, in the fourth carriage from the front. It could be devastating if some imposter came along to upset the dynamics by pinching your seat and you would be forced to spend the duration of the journey giving them the evil eye.

Oh, it was alright for the upstart, who would scamper off when we reached our destination, for a lovely care-free day, unaware that I would be spending my own day under a cloud of visceral infringement because I'd had to sit on the left instead of the right. But routine was what kept us going; it provided the safety rails that prevented us from falling away into the risky, uncharted waters of a more free-range existence.

My working life was not all drudgery of course. There were the monthly piss-ups after work and the lunches at the trattoria round the corner where we would embarrassingly count out our saved luncheon vouchers when it came to paying. Oh, and lets not forget the healthy payslips and bonuses that magically appeared at the end of each month. Yet even given these finer points of my working life I was still aware that there was something missing.

My artistic revelation had made me aware for the first time in my life (it takes me a while to cotton on) that actually I could take control and change things. This notion was admittedly born partly out of desperation to be doing something more creative and fulfilling and partly because my husband had strained the marital threads a bit too far and was auditioning for a role in 'Men Behaving Badly', so I felt little sense of loyalty towards him or the marriage. My mother had died a couple of years prior to this time, and I found that these life-changing events made me look at my own life more objectively.

I embarked on my new road in a small way by enrolling for an evening class, which fed my increasing desire to become an artist. I was still commuting up to London five days a week, but my enthusiasm/madness was so great that I signed up for an additional drawing class on Friday evenings after work, as well as the local one I was still attending, plus a painting class on Saturday mornings at St. Martins. I was gripped by the fever of a zealot; let's face it I must have been to travel back up to London on one of my precious days off.

The London classes were in a different league and I found myself in amongst the pro's, drawing nudes and sculls instead of egg boxes and flowers, but the tutors and fellow students were very encouraging and I was by this time starting to show promise. Still in the honeymoon period of my new life, I decided to apply for a full-time course in Graphic Design at Canterbury College of Art. When I announced my intention to my Saturday painting tutor he was quite upset and insisted that I was a painter rather than a designer. I don't know where he is now but he was proved to be right.

I had taken and obtained three O'levels courtesy of the Rapid Results correspondence course but I still didn't have the necessary educational requirements to get on to a foundation course, so a 2-year BTEC in Graphic Design was the closest thing I could get in order to fulfill my need to be drawing and painting.

Clutching a handful of drawings I took myself off to

Canterbury art college, after having arranged to meet Barry Kirk, who was the Vice Principal at that time, in order to get some advice. I will never forget the kindness and encouragement he showed me, nor the time he spent showing me around the college on that day, advising me how to go about applying for a place on the course.

It was a difficult time because I was still working full-time, going through a marriage break-up and sitting up half the night producing a body of work for my impending interview at the college. More than probably my obsession and determination to enter the art world kept me going through all this. I would draw anything; the house/garden/washing-up/friends etc. and well basically, anything that kept still for long enough.

When the day of the interview arrived I hadn't realized that I'd produced such an impressive amount of work of a reasonable quality, and I was told there and then that I had a place. I was so convinced that I wouldn't get in that I carried on for a bit, trying to prove myself, like a runner that keeps going after the race, until my interviewer had to tell me to stop, I WAS IN. I think I must have felt a bit cheated that I hadn't had the opportunity to say my party piece that I'd been rehearsing over and over again for several months previously, about giving me a chance etc. etc.

Little did I realize at that point, that I would later spend ten years of my life living with this man, or how important he would be in my development as an artist and as a person.

I had already gone through months of 'am I, aren't I doing the right thing?' so when it finally came, my exit from the world of season tickets and luncheon vouchers was relatively painless.

My workmates presented me with lots of packages individually wrapped up; paintbrushes, paints, pencils and canvasses etc. which accompanied by the bottle of gin we consumed, made me cry.

*   *   *

I spent the first five weeks at Canterbury in my year tutor's office bleating on about not being worthy/talented/young/bright enough to cope with the course – before the poor man finally lost patience, smacked his hand on the desk and said "For God's sake Wendy, stop making excuses and just get on with it". Whereupon I was so shocked that I worked my socks off for two years and finished up at the end of that time with a Distinction in Graphic Design.

Once I'd stopped being such a wuss and settled down to work, apart from some relatively minor problems (or perhaps small would be a more apt word), such as a flashing landlord and lots of teary phone calls from my now on the way to becoming ex, I loved my time at Canterbury.

It was a period of great change, which wasn't easy, but I was alive, excited and scared. I have never been so thin. I was also by this time, in love with my drawing tutor (as in interviewer). This was a complicated affair, but I believe the relationship made me work even harder to impress upon him and my family, who were bemused and suspicious by my new fervour, but most on myself, that I could transcend into the realms of actually being good at something.

My mother had died, as I have said, some years previously and my father could never in a million years comprehend how I could give up the security of my existing life in order to become in his words "a layabout /a hippy / deluded", after all, I had been working in the City, wearing smart clothes, and going abroad for my holidays; for someone who had started off with such low expectations of life I suppose I hadn't done too bad. BUT, the important thing, was that at last, at the grand old age of twenty eight, I was suiting myself.......and about bloody time!

The tutor/student relationship I was in, despite the fact that I was no Spring chicken, did throw up all sorts of, inevitably I suppose, prejudicial conjectures from other members of staff and I found myself having to work even harder to earn their respect, whilst my beloved would frequently send me out into the snow/rain/hurricane to draw and paint in an attempt to prove his impartiality. My fellow students didn't give two hoots and I enjoyed a great sense of camaraderie with them. In fact, because of my ancientness, I found myself acting as a kind of agony aunt for some of the younger ones; little did they realise it was the blind leading the blind.

I was steaming ahead on the right path now but I can't honestly say it was with great confidence. Having grown up believing that I was not really up to the mark, this notion was hard to shake off. However, I believe that a tricky childhood helped to give me strength and resilience and these, coupled with a sense of humour and sheer bloody-minded determination have been essential in my enduring ability to first of all hang-on during school years, then later to hang-in there as an artist.

As I was nearing the end of the course at Canterbury we had a career talk by one of the tutors. He gave us the low-down on the various colleges that those of us wishing to carry on with our studies might think about applying to, after this it was up to us to visit those we were interested in. At this time we were advised that as BTEC students we would be wise not to apply for certain colleges that were thought to be more for high-flyers, Brighton Poly being one of them, as priority would be given to Foundation students who were considered to be more elite............

*   *   *

My interview at Brighton didn't get off to a great start. I had dragged one of my sisters, who happened to be recovering from a slipped disc along, to provide moral chivvying and a spare pair of hands, and had booked us into a seedy but cheap B+B. This establishment, complete with stained carpets, artificial flowers and brown and soured cream paintwork was run by the typically clichéd seaside landlady, hair a curious shade of mauve, a fag stuck to her bottom lip and a cough that any miner would have been proud of.

After showing us to our room, which was a replica of the murder scene in 10 Rillington Place, and in between wheezing volcanic rumblings which kept threatening to erupt, she assured us that she would book a taxi for the following morning to ferry us to the college with all my clobber, for the interview.

Of course, as well as being an ugly old bag she was a liar and as a consequence of this, after a miserable plate of grease we left 'Sea View' (also a lie), and muttering our wishes that we hoped she would soon be front of house in that great guest house on the other side, we left, never to darken the door of her hovel again.

We finished up having to part run, (in Susan's case hobble) and part bus, with me screaming that we would be late. Oh for goodness sake, we could get her fixed up afterwards with some traction, but this was my chance at getting into Brighton, so my sister's vertebrae problems would have to take a back seat. In fact we arrived, albeit dishevelled, in reasonable time, due to my paranoia about being late, whereupon applicants were told to put up a small selection of their work in the limited space provided and the tutors would have a look first before calling us in individually for a grilling.

I have to say that Susan was not in the best of moods by this time, what with the fiasco of the journey and the fact that the tutor overseeing the candidates had just smiled at me and said "It's nice to have your mum with you isn't it". As there is only seven and a half years between us I could see why she wouldn't be best pleased and could only imagine the back problem had prematurely aged her.

Being the sort of person that tends to go over the top with things and because of the old paranoia about having to prove myself, I finished up presenting three times more work than I had been asked to. Having put up what I could, I also left a huge pile of drawings and paintings on the floor in a heap, as I ran out of time. My space looked like the contents of a skip.

We hovered around the corridors, Susan still sulking and me pacing like an expectant father in a 1950's film, slyly eyeing up the other candidates, smiling our perfidious smiles, and sipping our polystyrene coffee until it was time for me to hit the fan.

Interviews for college places then were much tougher than they are today. Remember this was before the days when universities have become so desperate to bring in more revenue that they will pluck someone in off the street, complete with shopping bags and offer them a place. Foreign students are even more desirable now, some of which can barely speak English, as they come with a higher booty.

Anyway, there were seven people on the interview panel, one of which was a student rep and another a Rotweiler. I felt the interview had gone quite well on the whole, except every now and then Mr meanie would chip in with a bastard question: "Why have you put Brighton down as your first choice?" I could hardly say I thought the night life would prove to be more interesting could I. This was immediately followed by "Why did you put Bath Academy down as your first choice, then change it to Brighton?" I tell you, Tippex, or Snowpake as it was called, was definitely inferior in those days and the ghost of Bath Academy loomed through underneath the cracked and flaky letters of Brighton Polytechnic to catch me out. They were lucky there was only one layer of white and not several other colleges vying for attention, given I'm the sort of person that takes half an hour to choose a packet of biscuits in the Co-op.

Afterwards when mum and I were stuffing the work away into various portfolios, the Rotweiler sidled up with a big grin (or maybe he was baring his teeth) and said "There, that wasn't so bad was it". I felt somehow that it was 'a sign', but by the time I had returned home to my garret in Canterbury, wasn't so sure and spent the next four weeks having apoplexy every time anything dropped on the mat.

The letter when it finally arrived, was opened under my instruction by my housemates ....I WAS IN.

*　　*　　*

My time at Canterbury had been a period of great change and growth. I had married very young and after all the upset of the break-up of this relationship I realised that we had both grown up and then apart. We were by this time on reasonably good terms and have remained so, albeit at a distance, ever since. In the meantime I had been busy falling in love with both my drawing tutor and Canterbury so the move to Brighton came as a huge wrench.

Now Art is definitely not a tidy business. As a result of this and coupled with the fact that I was an older student, so had accumulated more junk than someone just starting out would have, I came with enough clobber to furnish a small emporium.

This is when I discovered the true meaning of the

word 'tardis'. This was the name I gave to the flatlet that was to become my first lodging in Brighton. The tardis comprised an average sized bedroom in an ex council house, with a tiny sink and drainer, a single electric ring to cook on, a single bed and a two-bar electric fire.

On the day of the move, my new landlady, an indomitable woman of eighty-four who appeared to be wearing some kind of scaffolding under her cardigan, stood at the bottom of the stairs, stately as a galleon and frowning, whilst my friend and I staggered up to the tardis with about fifty loads that consisted of all my worldly goods. Every couple of minutes she would say incredulously "nearly there?" and I would try to reassure her by nervously laughing and saying "oh yes, just a couple more things". With every tread on the stair I could feel her dismay as she began to realise what she had let herself in for. She finally snapped when she spotted my stuffed bird peering jauntily out of the top of one of the boxes on the journey to his new home and announced with a quavering voice that she was going to put the kettle on.

When I asked Mrs Cooper what I should call her, thinking it would be one of those lovely old-fashioned names like May or Daphne, she visibly bristled and inflating her chest even more, announced firmly that she was 'Mrs C'.

On the whole, Mrs C (I never did discover her Christian

name) turned out to be not quite as scary as I'd imagined. She would get very worried if I ever showed her any artwork that I was working on in college and I discovered that the best I could hope for in terms of feedback was her being immensely relieved if she could recognise what it was.

I would wait until she had gone off to her daughter's in Rottingdean for the day, then like a naughty child I would marble paper, which is an incredibly messy business, in the tiny sink in the tardis, hang it on the washing line to dry, then quickly whip it all back in and clear up the mess before she returned.

If the air was a bit damp, I would have to dry the fruits of my labour in my room. How I never set fire to the place is beyond me. I had so much stuff in the space, some of which was dangerously close to the little electric fire.

Mrs C was a tough cookie, and tepid baths in the icy bathroom, along with drinking the cabbage water and one sherry with Sunday lunch, were according to the 'Mrs C book of wisdom', the main ingredients for longevity.

Like my mother, she took great delight in all things medical. After graphically regaling me one day with the finite particulars of her friend's prodigious bowel movements and the unfortunate ensuing surgery to correct the problem, she proudly went on to inform me that this person had convalesced under the capable eye of 'Matron C'.........in the tardis ....in my bed. Let me tell you, it is not always a blessing to have a vivid imagination. My little cot had been tainted. I would lay in bed, rigid, imagining all kinds of seepings into the space I had come to think of as my own. There had been a cuckoo in my nest that had deposited the stain of repugnance in my head.

Yet despite all this, Mrs C and I had survived my first year at Brighton art college together. We had even gone through the great hurricane of 87', where virtually the whole of Kent and Sussex had been decimated, but Mrs C's spindly little bird table in the back garden had stood proudly and resolutely unscathed the following morning. I remember getting up on that fateful night, to find Mrs C sitting in her armchair, looking a vision of loveliness in her blue brushed woollen dressing gown, with her hair-net in place, but minus her teeth, and how she excitedly told me "I thought there was a man under the bed"; how disappointing it turned out to be only the wind.

Yet I was starting to feel restless and confined, and began to hanker after some of the fun that my fellow students seemed to be having in their digs, like arguing about stolen food and whose turn it was to wash up. The crux came when I began to notice that I was only receiving telephone messages from those people that had been vetted and deemed suitable by Mrs C and the rest could just get lost.

I lived in three different lodgings during my time in Brighton. After getting tired of Mrs C intercepting my phone calls, I moved to a house on the other side of Brighton which I shared with a psychiatrist who was completely bonkers. I know they say that those in this profession need to go through therapy themselves in order to qualify them to help others, but she really did need help. Most of the time she was off her head on something or other that presumably she had obtained from the dispensary where she worked. Eventually that little chapter in my life came to an end when I began to fear for my life and felt the need to push a chest of drawers against my door each night as there was no lock on the door. Mrs C had already been promoted to an angel in my head and the seepings had faded to a dim stain; I'd only been gone a matter of months.

*　　*　　*

The relationship that I had begun in Canterbury with Mihangel, my drawing tutor, continued at a distance, so the opportunities for us to meet were few and far between. In some ways this probably wasn't such a bad thing because it meant that I was able to put my all into my work. I certainly wasn't well off but I was able to cope financially because of my working years as a civilian. Also it was before the days of the student loans, plus I received the full mature student grant and help towards my rent, so I was able to manage quite well. Ha ha, little did I realise at that time what was in store.

The BTEC course I'd done so well in at Canterbury had been very structured and the ratio of students to staff was small, so there was a lot of support and hand-holding (literally in my case). It came as a bit of a shock to discover then, that the Degree course in Illustration that I had embarked on in Brighton was so different. This was a much more mature approach to study where students were encouraged to be self-motivated and to think for themselves.

All this thinking was doing my head in and I have to admit I found this new approach to study quite difficult at first, but after a few months I began to settle down. We had some great tutors who would set us stimulating projects, at the end of which there would be a massive critique with all the staff and all the Illustration and Graphic Design students for that year. These sessions might go on for anything up to three days. They were incredibly nerve-wracking whilst your turn to have your work verbally torn to shreds loomed nearer, but once you had 'been done' you could sit back and enjoy some other poor sod being decimated. On reflection these critiques were wonderful. They were harsh but constructive and you learnt not only from your own thrashing but from everyone else's too.

The history of art department at Brighton was staffed

by some of the most inspiring people in that field and it was not unusual for students to clap at the end of a lecture.

During my second year at Brighton we got to choose from various short courses for our art history option and I was fortunate to select 'Landscape painting throughout history' as one of my choices. I say fortunate, because the tutor for this course was retiring, so I suppose he had little to lose in terms of professional credibility and this made the whole thing more relaxed and less predictable than it might otherwise have been.

He was a sweet man who would bundle a group of us into the 'minibus' each week and drive us out into the country to visit some dusty house or other with a few landscape paintings that had been passed down. Once we had dispensed of this formality we would get down to the really stimulating part of the trip by finding the nearest pub. I believe on one or two occasions we did actually make some comment about the works of art we had seen.

Notice I put 'minibus' in inverted commas. This is because a trip in this special van deserves proper attention. The latch on the back doors was broken, so if whoever was driving forgot to tie them up properly, they would fly open as soon as we began to gather speed, on one occasion resulting in one of the boys being thrown out. He did make a full recovery though, and I think back wistfully to those halcyon days before

'Health & Safety' came along to spoil our fun.

I was by this time a very old person in my early thirties, but the age gap between me and my contemporaries was not a problem. Probably because I felt I'd missed out in some ways in enjoying my childhood, I was determined not to be outdone, so have been on a mission ever since to try to recapture it in adult life.

At the weekends a little group of us would load up the ancient Citroen that belonged to one of the posh students whose parent's were well-off enough to buy him a car, and go off into the Sussex Downs to draw and paint. We did actually produce some quite nice spontaneous work during these excursions before we inevitably ended up in some pub or other. I remember the owner of the car with some fondness because he was a poser. He would turn up in a crisp white shirt, a cravat and a straw hat. I believe he is big in amateur dramatics these days.

We were like a family and propped each other up in times of stress.

*   *   *

Yuck, enough of the rose tinted stuff – blimey I can

almost see myself in a Laura Ashley frock standing at my easel, which just happens to be perched in a meadow – now, back to the harsh reality of downtown Brighton.

My last lodging in Brighton (I have saved the best one until last), was much closer to the college, which was great, as we artists have a lot to carry. OK that's the positive. It was a bed-sit in a grand Georgian house that had once been the home of Sir Stanley Gibbons, the chap that had invented the postal system, and it was part of a terrace that resembled the Crescent in Bath. During my time, it was owned by a 'Rackman' type landlord that none of the residents appeared to have ever seen and it was divided up into numerous bed-sits with a couple of shared bathrooms, the whole of which was maintained by a caretaker and his wife. Any delusions of grandeur I may have harboured on my initial visit, about residing at this dwelling, were quickly and rudely cut short however when I realised that things were not quite as they appeared to be on the surface.

I swear I am not making this up : The room below mine was inhabited by a prostitute and her pimp who would regularly beat the poor girl up. When she was with a client, the overhead light bulb would be red, then it would be changed to green when the coast was clear, ready for the next punter. Bully boy would go up to the phone box on the corner of the road to meet the next customer and bring him to the house, where he would lurk around the entrance hall until the mission was accomplished. My work ethic became seriously threatened for a while, as I was spending so much time spying on them, fascinated by the comings and goings; until BB leered at me one day when I was going out and I feared he might be measuring me up as a potential 'new girl'.

The top floor of the house was inhabited by the skateboard junkies. During my time there, they nicked the chandelier, which had been left from more salubrious times, the hall rug, the door knobs, and well, basically any inanimate objects that happened to be around. Any post that didn't look like a bill or circular was automatically opened to check for money, then thrown back down on the floor. Dubious, desperate characters would ring the bell throughout the night, presumably to get the next fix from the dealers upstairs.

The walls were not much more than partitions really. My immediate neighbour was a crack head and would arrive home in the early hours to put his telly on full-blast. I kept a tin of beans handy which I would use to bash on the wall in an attempt to quieten him down. Perhaps I should have tried custard or spam, as this rarely seemed to work. The parents, obviously unable to cope with him anymore, would come and scoop up his dirty washing once a week. His father, had some problem with his voice, and given my imagination, I worked out that he had had his tongue cut out by the Brighton mafia. If I hadn't been so bloody angry I more than probably would have thought how sad it all was.

I was much too frightened to use the shared bathroom at night which was just along the corridor, so I kept a plastic bucket under the bed that I shared with the mice. I know this is all sounding like a Monty Python sketch but apart from the bit about the mafia (they might hunt me down) this is all true. I hardly dare tell you about the Scottish couple that lived along the corridor and of how he would lock her in their room all day when he went to work if they'd had a row, although on reflection I suppose that could have been for her protection. Anyway, you probably can't take any more of this so I'll move on.

Whilst I was living in this establishment, I felt like I was in the middle of Piccadilly Circus. Apart from the sinister comings and goings within the house, there was a constant stream of fast moving traffic outside and the sound of sirens all through the night, not to mention the screams, presumably of people being murdered, emanating from the green across the road.

The obvious thing of course would have been to move, but I was in my final months at college, with a huge work load with its accompanying pressure and couldn't face the thought of finding somewhere else to live and going through all that again; plus I was aware that the experience might prove to be interesting dinner-party talk for when I had become a hugely successful artist, so I decided to stick it out. My father at this time, had confided to one of my sisters that he was afraid I had gone down the wrong path, and was convinced I had become a 'lady of the night', but friends informed me that this episode in my life was character-building. Yeah right!

Summer holidays were spent travelling to Wales with Mihangel, in an ancient van with a red dragon that he had painted on the side. In the early years, we would sleep in the back, along with all the art equipment that M had randomly thrown in. It was much more important to him, to remember to pack the fixative and charcoal than to worry about more earthly things such as coffee and soap, and I struggled vainly to maintain any sense of glamour on these trips.

After a few years of trying to apply mascara in a way which looked like I wasn't wearing any, and of removing congealed putty rubbers from my backside, I experienced great relief when he announced his intention to buy a house in Wales, which would provide a permanent base.

The course I was on was loosely structured, but gave me enough freedom to develop in the way that suited me, i.e. as a painter. These excursions to Wales ignited my love for the land and I would return to college at the end of the Summer armed with drawings and paintings.

The 3 years I spent in Brighton were hard, sometimes grotty, but overall, great. I feel privileged to have gone to Brighton Poly when it was in its heyday and I met some inspiring people, both tutors and students.

I know that a period of intense study is a life changing experience for anyone and by the time I graduated with a 2.1 in Illustration in 1990 I had metamorphosed into a very different person from the one that had worked in the City just five years earlier

PART TWO

CROESO I GYMRU

Wendy Murphy

There we are, a little bit of homework for you if you don't speak the lingo.

My long-distance relationship with Mihangel had progressed, but he was feeling an increasing need to get back to his roots in Wales. Now that he had made the commitment of buying a house, I was faced with another crossroads in my life, to live there or to settle down in England?

The consequence of this, and not without some considerable trepidation, I moved to North Wales in the same year that I graduated, to a virtually derelict farmhouse which dated back to Elizabethan times. M, was by this time running a Degree course in Kent during the week but doing a 300 mile round trip in order to come home each weekend.

The house was tucked away at the bottom of a valley between two mountains, with a little stream running along one side, and was situated on the edge of a tiny hamlet called Frog. I later learnt that it's real name was Friog, but some local joker had painted out the letter i. This kind of thing was obviously considered to be a hoot, because the nearest small town of Tywyn had also been tampered with and was known affectionately as Taiwan which admittedly lent a much more cosmopolitan feel to the place. Golly, what fun!

Isn't it amazing how one's perception of a place can alter, according to whether you are stuck there, up the creek without a paddle so to speak, or have the option of waving merrily as you drive away.

During the putty rubber years, when our en-suite had been a public toilet in whichever car park we happened to have spent the night in, despite the lack of comfort, I had been seduced by the spectacular drama and beauty of this part of Wales; the outcrops of rocks covered in heather and bright yellow gorse; great cascading waterfalls that reduced you to the size of an ant; waking up to the eerie sound of the curlews and oyster catchers that haunted the vast stretches of sand that formed the stunning Mawddach estuary; or looking out across Cardigan Bay towards the lonely shores of the Llyn Peninsular.

When it was time to say goodbye, we would have a final look in the rear view mirror to see the mountains diminishing into blue hazy humps as we sped on our way to the M54 and eventually Brighton.

Blimey, I wonder if I could get a job working for the Welsh tourist board?

There must be something in the old adage 'you always want what you can't have, because I had just spent the best part of five years dreaming of a time when I would never have to say goodbye to this corner of paradise again. Yet now that moment had arrived I was desperate to leave. A dense fog had rolled into my head, through which I could just about make out the shapes of everything that was wrong.

I was cold, lonely and living on a building site, oh and my father was dying. After the support and stimulation of being at art college in Brighton, I felt like an astronaut that had been cut loose.

I didn't have a car at this point, having only fairly recently passed my …. Erm….. fourth driving test. This achieved only after a series of hair curling experiences involving rolling backwards down a steep hill in Brighton, slapping an over enthusiastic instructor when he tried to put my leg into gear one too many times and who thought that all art students were layabouts; oh, and on one particular test, mounting the pavement. But hey, I only failed on that one little thing……

Anyway, by the time my beloved arrived home at some God forsaken hour each Friday night, completely knackered, I was chomping at the bit and desperate for sympathy, adventure and outings.

How could I have envisaged, when I was swanning around art college, imagining myself taking the art world by storm, that when I was finally spewed back into the real world, I would find myself not so much painting pictures, but hanging upside down like a bat, painting rotting beams, with anti-woodworm solution running down my arms.

This wasn't what I'd signed up for. I'd become used to living inside a warm cocoon of creativity; a world where someone would set me a project, which I would do to the best of my ability, then allow myself to be reassured by fellow students that "of course it isn't rubbish Wendy, take no notice of Professor Arnold – what does he know, just because he's Head of Art". But here I was in a foreign land, on my own for the best part of the week, with no-one around to massage my ego. Let me tell you, sheep really aren't up to much when it comes to giving a critical opinion and the best they could manage was 'baa' or the occasional meeer. Mrs C was beginning to look like John Ruskin in comparison.

Now, instead of trips to art galleries, museums and the cinema, I found myself looking forward to the highlight of my week, which was a trip to the local rubbish tip, in order to get rid of the latest pile of household detritus that had been left by several generations of previous residents in the house I pathetically called home.

At the weekend, Mihangel and I would load the dragon van up to the gills with chipped toilet bowls, three legged tables and dead cats, before setting off like hillbillies to the dump, where we would deposit it all, before loading up again with a new pile of, this time, someone else's crap.

We were like survivors of a nuclear holocaust, picking our way through the spoil-tips of other people's lives, which always seemed to be more interesting than our own.

Mihangel, particularly, could always see the 'potential' in that chair that had the seat missing, or that wooden box, whose lid we never did manage to prize open.

My heart would sink as I listened to his zealous ravings about how we were going to sand, paint, stain and wax. I tried to enthuse about his big plans to fill our home with all those unloved objects that we were going to 'distress' even more than they had been at the hands of their previous owners, before they were 'born again' and given the title of shabby-chic. I would secretly and wistfully think back to the days of Ikea, as we welcomed the newcomers into the fold of existing crap that was waiting in the growing queue of stuff that needed 'seeing to'.

It is hard to pinpoint which periods of my life have been the most miserable, but I believe this one was right up there with not being chosen to play one of Jesus' sunbeams when I was six, and discovering that the eleven year-old child that I overheard some older girls describing one day as 'that sweet little podgy one', was in fact me.

I had moved from a place where a typical headline in the local paper would read 'GANGLAND GRANNIE COOKS ERRANT SON ON FAMILY BARBECUE', to somewhere where the most exciting story of the week was 'MAN MOOVES IRATE NEIGHBOUR'S WHEELY BIN THREE INCHES' or 'TIDDLES FOUND IN GARDEN SHED AFTER TWO HOUR SEARCH'.

I spent the first three years living in Wales complaining that I hated the house, the place, the Welsh, the weather, the cold, the lack of decent shops etc. etc. No, I was far from ready at this stage to give in and remember that I had moved to one of the most beautiful areas on earth because I was far too busy telling everyone how much I hated the place, and swearing that I would only stay for five years maximum before going back to 'the mainland' and civilisation.

Twenty-seven years later I still appear to be here.

*   *   *

I believe a key factor in the slow start of my recovery from misery was the purchase of my first car. I will always have a special place in my heart for 'Bunty', my lovely little light blue Mini (being an artist, the colour of the car is obviously much more important than other more boring considerations such as engine size and whether it has been serviced recently). Bunty was a Mini-Mayfair so was a bit of a 'sloane' amongst cars. Ok, she'd been round the block a few times, but then so had I, so I felt we were made for each other.

Anyway, Bunty was my ticket to freedom. I could now enjoy and explore the beautiful landscape that I was beginning to re-discover and pick out through the gloomy fog that had taken up residence in my head, but more importantly I could go out and about photographing stuff that I could use as reference material for painting.

When Bunty was booked in at the local garage for treatment of one of the many illnesses she suffered throughout her twilight years, even the lads working on her called her by name and were quite tearful when she was finally given the last rights. Her successor, 'Joey', was also a Mini but was not a deluxe model this time. Although he served me well enough, me and the boys were never quite as attached to him.

The Mini years were great, except I was unable to go out when it was raining, as that distributor thingie that feeds the vital organs of the car, was positioned in such a way that it would attract complete saturation at the first sniff of any moisture in the air, whereupon the car would promptly die. As you will appreciate, living in an area which is not famed for its dry climate, I was grounded quite frequently. My friends at the garage, (I spent so much time there we became quite pally), devised a marvellous cover for this thing, involving a washing-up bottle and several rubber bands. Yet even this piece of ingenuity had it's limitations in Wales, and still I spent many a happy hour conked out at the side of the road. I could have taken shares out in DW40. I used to take a book out with me to while away the time I was spending 'drying out' and local folk would wave merrily as they passed saying "oh it's alright, it's that artist".

If I'd had the money I would have liked to keep a Mini as a pet. I am, I'm afraid, the sort of person that turns the music up in order to hide any funny noises the engine is making and feels immensely grateful if nothing has dropped off the car for a few weeks. I'm not proud of this, but I did once have a wheel drop off, when the wheel-bearing, which had been grumbling for some time, finally gave up the ghost.

Oh, I know I should be more responsible, but for heaven's sake I'm an artist and shouldn't have to bother myself with such prosaic matters; anyway, to be honest, any vehicle I've ever owned has been virtually knackered to start with, given that my finances, or rather lack of them, have only ever run to clapped out old bangers, so I was less likely to be precious with them.

I like to think of myself offering palliative care for cars that are one skid away from the knackers yard. From the car's point of view, spending their last few hundred miles with me must be like being in a very badly run nursing home.

Cars have featured big in my life since becoming an artist. Ferrying work around to various galleries, photographic sorties, and providing a get-away vehicle in dangerous situations. I have been chased by old ladies, farmers, cows, and on one occasion had a vicious dog set loose on me by an evil old harridan whose house I happened to be photographing. My screaming at her that I was an artist only seemed to fuel her anger and I scarpered by the skin of my pants, with the hound of hell hurling itself at the car.

The painting I did of her house was lovely though – Bllllltthhhhh!

I have had to be an opportunist and seize the moment on many occasions. Photographing or sketching someone is of course an invasion of their privacy but it is not always possible or preferable to ask permission, and if you want your subject to look natural its better to be sneaky.

I feel that artists need, and in fact often are, given special dispensation when it comes to this sort of thing; "yes, it's perfectly alright for you to do a quick sketch of that fit looking bloke opposite that you can just about make out with binoculars …… you're an artist".

*   *   *

I loved to paint flowers and on occasions boats and the sea, as I still do, but I was at this time, establishing myself as a landscape painter, although my landscapes were not empty, and I always seemed to feel the need to fill them up with rustic buildings, farm animals and old codgers, so it was important for me to feel at one with my surroundings. Remember I had been a townie though, so the idyllic illusion I'd carried in my head regarding the countryside, stemming back to the days of 'Pinky porker goes on holiday', was cruelly shattered when I realised that Pinky's holiday entailed a trip to the slaughter house.

One of the biggest things I have had to come to terms with living in the country is that it is full of, well .... Country stuff ...... like sheep getting stuck in barbed wire fences and lambs getting separated from their mothers. I once spent three and a half hours carrying a forlorn lamb around in my arms trying to find mummy. Oh, the little thing was happy as Larry, obviously enjoying what it considered to be a bit of a jolly, and would look up at me adoringly as I tried to cajole it to bleat every time we approached a likely candidate. According to the pink splodge on it's back, I could just about make out that it was no.14, but despite calling out 'no.14' each time we neared a maternal group, we were having no luck.

The one thing I have learnt, is that sheep are meanies and will not foster or adopt any children that they have not actually given birth to. Well, not unless you do all that business involving dead mothers (or is it lambs) and the tying on of skins and stuff, which I can assure you I've no intention of getting into. No, they will butt the impostor firmly out of town.

Anyway, when I couldn't take any more rejections, I was eventually forced to give up, and heartbroken, I put the little thing down close to where I had found it, whereupon it happily started munching as if nothing had happened. Even so, I was convinced that the next time I passed that way, I would see it half devoured by crows.

When I descended back down into the village, covered in grease and pink dye, I dug out the farmer where he was enjoying a leisurely pint in the local pub after a hard day up the mountain, and dramatically relayed my sorry tale, expecting him to rush to the scene of the tragedy. He, along with several other locals trying not to smirk, said wearily that he would sort it out in the morning.

He stopped me several days later and told me that mother and baby had been reunited and were both doing well.

I have to believe he was telling the truth.

My reputation as 'a country girl' was already shot to pieces by this time, as a result of a previous woolly incident.

During one of my walks, posing as a rustic local, with my sketchbook, muddy boots and shepherds crook, I had come upon a large ewe laying across the path in a rather awkward position, surrounded by other sympathetic females. There seemed to be quite a lot of groaning and grunting going on and peering closer I realized with a thrill that I could see the head emerging and that I was in fact witnessing a tricky birth.

During my search to let the farmer know, this is the same farmer from the lost sheep episode, I had time to contemplate how wonderful it was that the 'ladies' had been so supportive of their suffering friend, and marvelling at the compassionateness of nature, felt *touched* to have witnessed this woolly maternity club, although I must say I thought the farmer might have shown a bit more gratitude when I eventually found him, instead of just grinning at me.

Several days later I heard how well the story had gone down in the pub about the large well-endowed ram that had apparently given birth to his own balls.

These pathetic attempts to bond with nature and prove myself as a local, kept backfiring; in fact all they seemed to be doing, was to prove to the natives that I was, as they had suspected, a townie twerp.

Oh where were the solo exhibitions, where were the features in leading art magazines and the requests for me to appear on daytime TV with my latest masterpieces.

Five years at bloody art college, and here I was, agonizing over whether to draw the sheep with woolly hats on or just stick to the sheepdog wearing Wellingtons, for the sheepdog trials poster I'd been asked to do.

Didn't these people realise I was out; I was ready; I'd arrived. I was a newly fledged swimmer, standing in a pool where all the water had been drained out. I had crawled to the top of my little pedestal, only to find the arrows all pointing downwards when I got there.

The trouble with living in a small rural community, is that once the locals get wind of the fact that you are an artist, they will spend every waking moment dreaming up new ways to test your creative skills, not to mention your sanity; posters for bingo, gardening competitions and tractor races; knitting fests, best looking horse and children's art competitions; all requiring artwork from you know who.

If you try to wriggle out, all you get is "what do you mean, you don't do that sort of work, you're an artist aren't you?". One smock fits all.

For God's sake, how was I ever going to be allowed to believe that my work was that of a great genius, if I was constantly being asked to do pictures of Noddy and Big-ears or funny men holding up pneumatic onions.

Things came to a head eventually, when I was asked to help paint a mural on the toilet walls of the local infant school. It was the pathetic little jokes about being 'flushed with success' and being told that I could do the job 'at my own convenience', which finally made me realize that I would have to choose between being a 'serious artist' or 'a pillar of the community', if my career wasn't to slide slowly down the pan.

The positive to be found in any situation where you feel yourself to have gone to the skids and are at the bottom of the muck pile, is of course that you can only go one way ………

Talking of muck piles and whilst I'm still on country matters, I feel duty bound to confess to you my cow problem. Yes, I have a healthy respect for cows. I won't walk through a field if there is a cow on the horizon.

Don't get me wrong, I love animals, including our bovine friends. BUT, for some, I admit irrational reason, I am convinced that I will be one of the miniscule percentage of the entire population of Britain, that once every eight years or so, suffers death by cow.

A couple of married artist friends and I often go on arty soirees and will testify that I have taken us on some terrifyingly dangerous detours to avoid these gentle creatures; over barbed wire fences, down ravines, where on one occasion the entire contents of our picnic bag rolled out and ended up in a watery grave at the bottom. (They've never forgiven me for that one). On another occasion I climbed the fence and took refuge in an electric sub-station in order to escape a quietly grazing herd.

It's amazing how athletic one can become when under pressure. On one old school report the teacher had written "Wendy would do much better if she were prepared to take her feet off the ground". I like to think how proud she would be of me now.

The ironic thing is, that I have painted cows on lots of occasions. I have herds of them at home stuffed away in files, along with my own flock of sheep, stormy seas and derelict cottages.

*   *   *

When I had been living at the farmhouse for several years, Mihangel and I were both short-listed as prize-winners in the National Eisteddfod. This is the event in the Welsh calendar where local bank managers and the like, get togged up in their wive's best table linen, and compete against each other for various prizes in the fields of poetry, singing and in more recent years the visual arts; culminating in the lucky recipient of the top prize for poetry being awarded the 'bardic chair'.

It's a bit like a TV talent show, but instead of the winner getting a cash prize or a record deal, they get a …. chair.

I'm really sorry, but I am going to have to apologise now for attempting to get a cheap laugh by trivialising this ancient event, which is very much part of the Welsh culture.

51

To be fair, the said chair is quite a large and impressive affair; all carvings and what not, although in all honesty I can't really see how it would go down with the rest of the family once it was in situ, next to the sofa from DFS, but there we are. "Elaine, move the washing airer out of the way love, I want to make room for THE CHAIR"; "Dean, get that bloody table top football out of the way, I want to put THE CHAIR there".

You can see that a piece of furniture that looks like it's heralded from Windsor castle, might not fit that well in your average semi.

Anyway, enough of home furnishings. The visual arts at the Eisteddfod are displayed in a large marquee, which as you step through the tent flap, magically transcends into a slick white gallery.

The whole caboodle is a prestigious affair, and Mihangel, as a proper Welsh bloke, and me, as an English 'blow-in', felt very honoured to be part of this event. We were particularly chuffed, as we had also been asked to take part in a television programme featuring a small selection of that year's participants. My God! At last, this was it; we were going to be celebrities ..... the Richard and Judy of Gwynedd; today Frog, tomorrow the world ...... I hadn't felt this sort of nervous anticipation since the maypole went missing in the Archers.

On the day of the filming, our faces glowed with

shame as we nervously hovered, watching the small but charming film crew rearrange our home in order to make it 'camera friendly', exposing several years worth of filth under mats and items of furniture that we'd 'gone round' on those rare, occasional bouts of housework.

After spending the morning being humiliated and exposed as filthy sluts, we were told cheerfully that the filming would take place outside, presumably in order to protect their expensive equipment from contamination.

Our beloved, but 'characterful' sheepdog Megan (they're all called Megan around here), had been sent off with her box of Shapes, to spend the day with aunty Lillian, our neighbour just up the road, and was in a real strop at not being allowed to run amok amongst the tripods or round up the film crew (the dog that is, not Lillian).

In keeping with the Welsh fascination for chairs, Mihangel's entry for the exhibition had been three beautiful Welsh stick chairs which he had carved with a single Stanley blade, then hand painted, stained and waxed, so it was appropriate that he should be depicted at his rustic Black & Decker workbench, pretending to chop a piece of wood, for the film.

Without wishing to re-open old wounds, the best way I could describe his performance on that day would be to say that if he had been auditioning for a part playing the 'angst artiste' in an August Strindberg play, he would have walked it.

To be fair, he had been quite accommodating initially; moving the wood to the left 2cms; moving it back to the right 1mm; moving it so that the top right hand corner was facing just a tinsy bit more towards the camera man; raising the axe-wielding hand a little higher; then a little lower; bringing it down fast; then in slow motion; then slow but slightly faster as in Mihangel's imagination it came crashing down into Chris Sear, the presenter's skull.

Meg, having been listening from Lillian's garden, picked up with her doggie antennae, daddy's raised voice, as he refused point blank to do 'take 18', and joyously joined in with a spate of excited barking, before she had to be dragged back inside with edible bribes, after the sound man screamed "for God's sake someone shut that bloody dog up".

I, on the other hand, was a natural, but then I had spent the previous two months practicing in front of the mirror upstairs, so I was virtually word perfect by the time of my debut performance.

The setting for the interview where I was to talk about my paintings, was in the paddock, just a short distance from the house, and despite feeling that I had been given the same status as a horse, I reeled off my little soliloquy with the ease of an Oscar-winning actress.

I was a bit disappointed that I hadn't been asked to do an action shot or seventeen of me painting, but I think the crew were feeling a bit wary by this stage, after the histrionics of Mihangel's performance. I also felt rather miffed that the actual time I'd had in front of the camera was so short, and that I hadn't had the opportunity to flounce out of the paddock (I've always wanted to flounce) – but then I suppose less can be more when it comes to greatness.

There was obviously some glitch in the cutting room afterwards, because when we finally saw the programme when it was televised, seven and a half hours worth of toil had been reduced to four and a half minutes of film, showing the artists in their natural habitat, accompanied by Michael Nyman with music from 'The Piano' and the distant barking of Megan the dog.

This brush with showbiz made me wonder if perhaps I shouldn't have followed in the footsteps of other great divas and become a 'prima-donna' – yet when I really stopped to think about it, if I was ever going to consider yet another change of direction in my career, it would have to be in a very different area to the Arts, if I were ever to locate any semblance of 'normality' in myself – and I'd already tried that hadn't I, so I was back to square one.

*   *   *

Actually, I believe that I may have missed my true vocation and should in fact have become an estate agent instead of an artist. Not only would I have got paid for the work, but I really do have a fascination for houses. I find it very difficult to paint a landscape without plopping some sort of dwelling into the picture. I have a reputation among local art groups of being 'the queen of cottages' and can magically turn a three bedroom council house into a rustic dwelling.

This brings me on to the subject of what a shifty lot us artists are.

When I say that I can perform miracles by turning a modern house into a hovel I am not exaggerating. If I had to describe myself since becoming a painter, I would say that I have learnt to become a voyeur, a thief, a liar and a cheat. I study my prey and steal a moment in time, then twist and turn it into whatever I want it to be.

I could sit down for thirty years and attempt to copy the view/tree/cottage/still life in front of me, but what would be the point. I might save myself the bother and take a photograph which would give me exactly that in a thousandth of a second.

I realised a long time ago that if I wanted to be

creative, I would need to add something or embellish my subject in some way, and the thing that I add is me, my personality, my thoughts and feelings. Of course photographers do this as well, but they can also produce an image which is a replica of what they have seen.

I see my own work as theatre; a subjective dramatization of the familiar, whereby I gather often unrelated elements, like cows and cottages and stormy skies, things that have stimulated me in some way, throw them all up in the air, then reassemble them in a way which I find more satisfying.

*   *   *

When I first moved to Wales I found myself working in a much more cautious way than I had whilst I'd been in Brighton. This was partly because my confidence was at a low ebb at this time, but also that I was, I believe, subconsciously doing things to try to please other people. I wanted to fit in and be accepted in my new environment. BIG MISTAKE. I was making assumptions about what I thought others would like, but more importantly I was allowing my work to become diluted.

I believe that artists need to be selfish and single-minded in their approach to their work if they are to maintain integrity and produce work which comes from the heart.

It's a tricky one really, because although this is what I believe, I am still like other mortals in that part of me craves the praise and admiration of those around me; the pat on the back. But I know that if I am to be true to myself, I will never hear those magic words: "Cor, that's brilliant love, you can see every hair on that dog's head", or "Look Doris, it's so good it looks like a photo".

But let's be honest, it's all very well sticking to your principles, providing you can find a market for tie-dyed road-kill. Of course having lack of financial restraint gives us the freedom to 'play' and to explore unfamiliar territory, so if like many artists, you struggle financially, you can find yourself in a moral dilemma.

I found myself faced with the choice of either compromising the type of work I wanted to do and producing nice little potboilers that my sister would approve of "you know, the type of thing people want to take home after their holiday" or of sticking to my guns and doing the work I wanted to be doing. I'm not saying that I want to tie-dye a dead squirrel, or that there is anything wrong with holiday potboilers, but they are just not what I want to do. The way round this problem for me has been to do all sorts of other ghastly jobs that have enabled me to follow my heart (more of these later).

The paintings that have transcended the test of time, have without exception been done by artists that have depicted the world through their unique and personal vision; work where the artists have not merely been a slave to the subject matter but have had something to say about it.

I am not decrying work which looks highly realistic, just because it isn't my way. There is more than one way to skin a cat, or a squirrel for that matter, and there is no one way of producing art that is the only, or right way of doing things, but the approach that an artist takes with their work, should I believe, be a reflection of what they are about, rather than that they are attempting to please Aunty Doris.

Anyway, you can forget family members, they're a dead loss when it comes to buying your work. No, stick to your guns and just accept that art appreciation is like fine wine and classical music, an acquired taste, but also that it is subjective.

The danger for amateur artists just starting out is that the 'aunty syndrome' can actually hinder their creativity if they allow it to, by undermining their confidence when it comes to having an open mind and willingness to experiment and take creative chances. No one wants to get home from having just spent three hours labouring over a painting in an art group, to hear their loved one say "yes luvvie, very nice, but you haven't put the white van in that always stands outside that cottage" or "why on earth have you painted that cow red"?

'Aunty syndrome' is less of a problem these days for a crusty old pro like me that has been in (that's in not on) the game for quite a long time, as I have become fairly impervious to it by now.

As well as learning to become liars and cheats, artists also have to be very sneaky people. Anyone that draws complete strangers whilst they are sleeping, eating, waiting for the bus, having a quiet drink in the pub or whatever, understandably will need to employ more than a hint of subterfuge if they are to get away with doing it undetected.

A small sketchbook hidden behind an open book on your knee or under the table is the answer. Once again, family members are a waste of time. As soon as you start drawing your loved one, that incidentally has been in a deep drugged coma for the last two hours, some six sense infiltrates their brain, the eyes snap open and they are off quicker than a whippet at Catford stadium.

Yes, I would say that family are definitely the most uncooperative when it comes to sitting for you, even for ten minutes. Even pets, that have sat looking at you adoringly, slope off to another room as soon as they glimpse the moving pencil. Either that or they suddenly need desperately to be sitting on top of your sketchbook and nowhere else will do.

Shunned then by nearest and dearest as being a 'bloody nuisance', I am doomed to a life of solitary confinement in my chilly garret. Obviously my time up the rope prepared me well for becoming the painting pariah that I am; not quite one of the team still, a bit on the edge. To be perfectly honest, I think these days I quite enjoy this feeling; it makes me feel perversely stronger than I might if I were being socially propped up.

Artists do sometimes work in groups or with friends, but the danger of this is that owing to the gentle and sensitive nature of us artists, we don't like to offend our fellow companions, so finish up patting each other on the back and telling each other how wonderful we are, so that in the end you begin to lose your critical judgement and start to believe it.

In order to remind myself that I am still part of the human race and to feed the part of me that is, dare I say it, actually quite sociable, I venture out of my cupboard sometimes and try to kid myself that I am really one of the crowd. An artist friend of mine was once described by a shrink as being a gregarious introvert. I can relate to that. The biggest thing that has helped me make this marriage between bohemia and civi-street has been to enter the word of teaching.

Wendy Murphy

MISS

Wendy Murphy

I had settled down to life in Wales, albeit reluctantly, but I was with the person I wanted to be with and very gradually started to make my life here. It wasn't easy because part of me was still fighting the loss of the buzz of living in a busy place. I missed the shops and the pressure and excitement of being among like-minded people that I'd enjoyed while I'd been at college. No doubt all graduates go through this transition period but I felt mine was more extreme because in effect I had moved to a different country with its own culture.

As I have said, the arrival of Bunty made a big difference, but I believe the greatest factor in determining not only my acceptance of living here, but of me actually embracing it, has been getting into teaching.

Now I will be the first to admit that the business of teaching can be, and often is, a pain in the arse. It is exhausting, can be frustrating and you can more often than not find yourself in the position of having to play amateur psychologist (more about nutty artists later).

The upside is that there is satisfaction and fulfillment to be had from the feeling that you might have played even a small part in helping someone on their way or of making something a bit clearer for them. On a more selfish level, teaching has helped me enormously with confidence issues. You can't be worrying about what you sound or look like when faced with a sea of hungry, not always friendly, faces, so that in the end you start to worry about them rather than you and you move up a few notches on your personal scale of self-belief, when you remember that you have come face to face with the terror of entering the piranha pit of students and lived to tell the tale.

The other big thing that teaching has provided me with is a whole network of other people that like me, have been crazy enough to want to embark on the journey along the creative road.

I have taught for over twenty-five years and in most capacities; adult education evening classes, painting holidays, private tuition, workshops and short courses, and for the past seventeen years have been a part-time lecturer in Life Drawing and on occasions Painting at the local tertiary college.

You may be thinking Blimey, when did she get time to paint through all this, but I have only ever taught in a part-time capacity so have always managed to maintain a balance between doing my own work and working for someone else. Lets face it, if I'd been teaching, or for that matter painting full-time during these years, I'd more than probably be rocking gently backwards and forwards in a home by now.

During this time I can boast that I have lost a student, (in fact I've lost several during outdoor sorties, or maybe it's more accurate to say that they've managed to shake me off). I did hit a student once but I'm not prepared to go into that one …….. Oh for heavens sake it was only that one time. But my piece-de-resistance was when I killed a student. Ok I said that for dramatic effect. I didn't actually kill him, well not directly anyway, but the poor man did expire during one of my workshops. I had taken the quite elderly group that this man was with, out for a day's painting at a local sea-side resort …..and well yes, it was quite chilly ….. and OK, I admit I had kept them out for quite a long time …… but blow it, I was determined they were going to produce some worthwhile work to take back to the studio, before they were locked up for the night.

I had mistakenly thought the tinge of blue around this poor man's mouth was a smudge of cobalt that he'd been using for his sky, so I was mortified when we arrived back at the studio and he suffered a fatal heart attack and died.

Some cruel friends at the time suggested that I might like to think about running coffin-making courses for the elderly; you know the kind of thing, arrive in your own car and travel home in your hand-made box; there may even have been some potential in doing a deal at the local garage re. the redundant cars, but I couldn't face it in the end and in reality it was a ghastly experience and very upsetting. *

*If you would like to book a workshop with me I can be contacted via e-mail.

*   *   *

This unfortunate incident happened during a stint of working for an art-holiday enterprise. The painting holiday episode lasted about seven years and it was my introduction to the world of teaching.

Although I had spent five years at Art College I was in no way equipped to teach and quite frankly I was petrified. My own chosen medium was oils but of course these students, virtually without exception, wanted to work in watercolour. My skills in this area were limited to say the least and I spent my first teaching sessions rifling through a 'How to Produce a Watery Masterpiece in a Week' book, that just happened to be laying open on my upstairs studio floor, then running back downstairs to relay the latest find to my unsuspecting students, before dashing back up for the next installment.

Actually I must have picked up a few tips, because without wishing to blow my own trumpet, oh go on then, I went on to be a runner-up in the Sunday Times Watercolour competition a few years later.

Used to working in oils, I decided to treat my entry into this prestigious competition in the same way that I would normally handle a painting i.e. by laying the paint on with a trowel. I believe I even incorporated a little household emulsion into my masterpiece (well it is water-based). I realised that admitting to this crime against traditional watercolour had not been a good idea' when the rather stuffy Arts correspondent from the newspaper in question, interviewing the winners at the time, for the article that was to appear in the supplement, sounded horrified by my admission and said "I don't think you have entered this competition before madam have you"? Later, when reading the published article, I saw that he had gone on to describe my submission as "A lively little picture. My painting was 4ft square so I can only assume his use of the word little was a put-down.

Anyway, going back to the business of painting holidays. This establishment was owned by a man that had taken early retirement from a career in advertising, then spent two years going on painting holidays, learning the ropes and pilfering as many tips as he could before setting up his own 'painting paradise'.

Funny really, that he should want to take on such a venture, because he didn't particularly like people. He managed to keep reasonably polite during the day, (well, most of the time), but come 8pm in the evening when the weary workers wanted congeniality and alcohol, he would promptly lock the bar, put the latch down on the front door and padlock the five-bar gate at the end of the drive before retiring to his quarters.

Now I admit that the small Welsh town that housed this establishment, lets call it 'D', was not at that time a great hub of interesting and exciting recreational activity, but damnit! these people were on holiday and would at least have liked the opportunity to discover this fact for themselves.

I had not realised at the time of accepting the job that part of my remit would be to work as a co-conspirator in organizing escape parties for the inmates. These were mainly genteel, retired professionals that had the wherewithal to go on these rather expensive, all inclusive holidays, so the sight of them clambering out of windows, running like escaped convicts up the drive, then hauling themselves over the gate to freedom, was incongruous to say the least.

I believe the delights of 'D' were considered much more of a prize than they might have been had not the naughtiness of the expeditions been so great.

I daren't divulge the jailor's name in case I am sued. He was a competent artist, could be kind, and on occasions, good fun. But he was dogmatic in his stubborn refusal to waiver from his strict routine and could be unbelievably petty at times. I remember one man once had the temerity to ask if he could take a knife out in his lunch box to cut up his apple and was categorically told 'NO'! It was a cheap stainless-steel variety, not one from the family silver.

The purpose-built studio was furnished in Magnolia with a beige carpet for God's sake (beige and art should not be in the same room together) and on more than one occasion I witnessed some elderly person on their hands and knees scrubbing frantically at some miniscule mark in order to avoid the wrath of the great man.

I heard him bellowing one day, at a very sweet lady that had been disobedient enough to have opened a small window in the stuffy studio, "God heats the outside – I heat the inside, and I don't want all that energy going out the window".

I grew strangely fond of both him and his very hardworking wife who organized all the non-artistic aspects of the place, which was well, everything really; from catering, cleaning and bookkeeping, not to mention pacifying those guests that her husband had upset during the day.

On the whole, the residents were competent people that were used to being good at what they did, so it often came as bit of a shock to those that had taken up Art in later life to discover that it was not, as they had imagined, something that flowed miraculously from the fingertips.

They had everything from fifty quid sable brushes, waterproof sketchbooks and easels that you could sit at, cook your dinner and paint a picture on simultaneously. The only thing that was quite often missing was any artistic ability. Some of them had been at it for forty years, by which time you'd think the penny would have dropped. I sometimes wonder at all the hobbies they might have excelled at instead; origami, macramé, white water rafting ....

Of course some were talented artists that had managed to produce some excellent work whilst maintaining demanding careers in other fields, but these seemed to be few and far between.

*   *   *

One of the hardest things for any would-be artist to get to grips with is the idea that they don't have to be a slave to their subject matter. As artists we are not just allowed to lie and cheat but are in fact positively encouraged to. The more timid minded may prefer to think of it as using 'artistic license'.

Once an artist realises that they can change the world, they are halfway there to becoming truly creative and to not being stuck with simply copying what they see. I don't wish to sound like a megalomaniac but who else do you know that can get up in the morning and decide to have a red lawn or a pea-green sky. We can turn our world into anything we want it to be.

I have always encouraged my students to lie and cheat. On one occasion during my time at the painting holiday establishment I had taken a very small group of students back to the decrepit farmhouse I called home and encouraged them to have a go at bringing out all its bucolic charm in their pictures. Now as I have already mentioned, this ancient house was straight out of a Thomas Hardy novel, complete with tiny crooked windows, alarmingly undulating roof eaves and flaking lime-washed walls.

Having just spent one and a half hours giving a lecture to the group on the merits of using artistic licence and exaggerating the characteristics of their subject matter, I was flabbergasted to find one of the men, a retired draughtsman, perched on his fishing stool, meticulously squaring up his drawing of the place with a 2H pencil and ….. wait for it ……a ruler, and was determinedly attempting to turn this rustic dwelling into a Barrat starter-home.

I understandably felt compelled to make an example of this sinner, so gathering the group together and finding a garden trowel, I ceremoniously buried the offending implements in a nearby flowerbed. Once he'd recovered his speech, this little exercise seemed to do the trick as I had him and his companions eating out of my hands for the rest of the week.

You are probably thinking I was a bit harsh and that I should have embraced his personal approach to drawing, but he had stressed on several occasions his desire to loosen up and move away from the confines that his working life had imposed on him.

I myself am a very loose woman. A framer I once had informed me that I had a reputation for being 'fast and loose'. The only trouble is I can't quite remember if I was wearing my civilian hat or my artistic one at the time.

Most of the work for the art holiday enterprise was done outside, during sorties into the surrounding countryside. I would start off by giving an hour-long lecture at the guest-house before we set off for the day with our packed lunches (minus knives). In order to avoid loss of resident and confusion I would ask them to allow me to go first and to lead the way. There would always be someone who couldn't wait and would either get horribly lost, (in the case of one woman not reappearing again until the evening, although it's possible she might have been trying to shake me off), or they would arrive at the destination thirty minutes ahead of everyone else. Either way it was my fault. It became a regular sight seeing little Bunty leading a procession of Rovers, Rolls Royce's and four wheel drives along the country lanes of Gwynedd. Considering the size of their engines they drove like snails, mainly at 15 miles per hour, slowing down to 10 if I tried to get them moving by speeding up a little.

Working en plein-air is fine providing all the conditions are perfect, which is …… well …… never. If not, I discovered that as their leader, I would get blamed for:

wind blowing sand or radio-active fallout from the nearby nuclear power station onto them, or worse, their work; hungry midges; them forgetting their favourite paintbrush; it being too hot/too cold/too wet/too dry/too windy, too far etc. etc.

One artist friend I know had plonked a group of students in a secluded field, whereupon a farmer came along on his tractor and promptly sprayed them with anti-fungicide before they could gather up all their clobber and move. Although it has to be said that none of them suffered with blight that year.

I would naively start off by asking the group not to set up their flimsy portable easels across too broad an area, which of course they completely ignored and resulted in me having to do a 2-mile hike between each one. Then I would be blamed for not getting round to them often enough.

On one occasion an ex-major type came puffing up to me and said "If you don't mind me saying miss (I liked that bit) I think you should get your group in order", as if we were on maneuvers.

But I think the most annoying lot were the people who would rabbit away over the top of me if I was trying to explain something to them. I very nearly shoved one woman into a fast-flowing waterfall once, when I was attempting to give her some constructive advice regarding her painting; "yes but I did it like that so that I could go over it all again afterwards when I'd done it wrong and I meant to use that really dreary brown because I was showing how the water makes those big ripples against the grass that I've put at the sides to show how it's framing those big rocks that I've made look like potatoes and I wanted to make the waterfall look like it's been cut off at the bottom with a pair of scissors rather than that it's flowing when it hits the bottom and I've ....

SHUT UP! SHUT UP! SHUT UP! ....just SHUT UP!

Sorry, I'm just having a sit down for a minute.

This day particularly stands out in my memory as being full of special delights; from the Mrs-I-know-it-all-better-than-you, to the swarms of midges that raged war on us all and for which I got blamed, to the lovely elderly gentleman that was desperate for me to share his flask of coffee from the cup that I had just seen a dew drop from his nose fall into.

*   *   *

Workshops in general are alright, providing the subject for the day is tutor-friendly. The one to really avoid though, is STILL LIFE.

The nightmare begins about a week before the

appointed day, whereby you have to start gathering enough clobber to open a junk shop. It's amazing how pathetically small all this stuff looks when it's spread over three tables in a large village hall. Once you have raided your own and several other people's houses and loaded the booty into various bags and boxes, your car looks like you've done a house burglary and you pray you aren't stopped by the police en-route.

The fun really starts though once you have arrived at the hall, have unloaded it all again and are desperately trying to concentrate on arranging three separate still-lives simultaneously in a limited space of time. All the while being accompanied by a cacophony of "darling, how are you", "can I just show you what I've been doing" and giving you the latest update on their daughter's (whom you have never met) amazing New York trip, (I've not had a holiday for 100 years), their husband's gall stone operation (who wants to know), and their own month-long stay at an idyllic retreat in Tuscany (what can I say).

Is it any wonder that one lady once unkindly likened my still-life to a car boot sale.

I was asked fairly recently to do a 'Flower Painting' workshop for an art group ……. in October for God's sake. Any subject that requires the use of natural material, is generally not great news, partly because you've got to try to keep the stuff alive, and partly because if the time of the year they want you to do it has an 'R' in the month, you will be hard pressed to find anything suitable, and on this occasion I was convinced that someone had it in for me.

Local people are used to seeing me wandering listlessly around the lanes at these times, with a pair of scissors and a bag, but there is only so much you can do with Ragwort. Those attractive weeds with the little pink flowers, so fresh and pretty, will I assure you, look like something the dog has sicked up after it's been eating grass, by the time you arrive at the hall.

The garden sorties of course have to be done after nightfall. I usually take an accomplice along with me for these, to keep cavy while I do a spot of neighbourly pruning. (I'm thinking maybe I should start charging).

Anyway, on this particular occasion, owing to the seasonal deficiency of stealable flowers, it meant that the 'meat' of the session was reliant upon members of the group themselves bringing in various blooms, such as could be found in October. (Remember that I am a starving artist so could only run to a couple of bunches of Chrysanths from the Co-op).

Well, let me tell you, they came in droves, bearing the most beautiful Autumnal flowers that any harvest festival show would have been proud of. I'd had the brainwave of setting up three different tables with a different colour scheme for each, which members of the group promptly set about dismembering when they arrived, so that they could steal the vases for their own contributions. I actually had a tug of war with one woman (you know who you are Dorothy). The day went remarkably well, considering. The group seemed to quickly forget that my opening words to the little introductory talk I gave them had been "don't ever ask me to do this again". Let's face it they probably won't after this.

A certain amount of rivalry goes on between the various art societies and you have to tell each group when you are with them that they are better than the other group just down the road. No, in fact they are better than any of the other art societies in the whole of Gwynedd.

Woe betide you if you bump into one of them on the street and accidentally mix them up and place them in the wrong group. They all know me, because well, there's only one of me, but despite the fact that there are hundreds of them I am expected to know instantly which society they belong to, but not only that, I also have to remember their names. They all seem to look the bloody same. Many's the conversation I've had with someone where the person has said "how are you Wendy?" whilst I'm frantically thinking 'who are you'? Yet it is possible I've discovered, to keep the pretence going for quite a while. If you can manage to keep the conversation on the general, rather than specific's, you stand half a chance of getting away with it. Of course the sensible thing to do would be to just admit to your loss of memory, but that would tell the person that they are so unmemorable and unimportant that you had forgotten all about them. The trouble with me is I'm too considerate.

I have on occasions been able to use the jealousy that exists between rival groups to advantage. In fact local art tutors owe me big time for the turnaround in the quality of refreshments offered during tea-breaks. Gone are the days when you would be lucky to get a weak coffee and a digestive.

The idea of playing the groups off against each other came to me when I was offered a piece of cake with my drink during one particular workshop I was doing. Ok it was only Mr K but nevertheless it was an improvement on the boring biscuit. On each successive day after this, that I spent in various enemy camps, I made sure that I casually mentioned some delicacy or other that I had enjoyed whilst teaching behind enemy lines, exaggerating the delicious factor of the proffered refreshment. Over a period of time I began to notice that the digestives had been replaced by jammy dodgers, then chocolate bourbons. Then the cakes started moving up from the Co-op's own budget range to M & S coffee and walnut.

These days, no self-respecting art society in this area will bring out anything other than home-made cake at half-time. During my last workshop I smiled, as a fabulous gateau was proudly produced during afternoon tea-break …….. I'm thinking I need to work on lunch ideas next … and a glass of Prosecco would help the creative flow …… oh, I wonder if it might be an idea for the students to have one too?

*   *   *

I have found there are a few things that have the potential to throw a hefty spanner in the works whilst doing a workshop. The first one is the 'late arrival'.

This is the person who arrives approximately twenty to thirty minutes late, (just long enough for you to have started your talk and to have got into your stride). The latecomer will then make a big show of apologizing and going into great depth regarding the reason for their lateness, whilst waving and mouthing hello's to their friends in the group. Just as you start to regain your equilibrium and have managed to remember what you were saying, this person starts unpacking their bag, and all you can focus on is the sound of them rummaging, whilst they are maintaining a whispered conversation with their neighbour.

One artist I know was so furious once, when he found himself in this situation yet again, that he stopped talking, packed his bag and went home. I would dearly love to be in a position to play Prima Donna, but my lust for the cheque at the end of the day always gets the better of me, so I find myself smiling through gritted teeth and assuring them that it's fine, and that I really hadn't got very far anyway. Bastards!

I have found another thing that can throw me off course when I'm faced with a group of people, is THE MAN IN THE ROOM ......This is the equivalent of the elephant but with only two legs.

Let me explain:

I went to an all girls school and I was brought up in a predominantly female household, with three sisters (well, two and a half really, but I'm not going into all that), and parents whose idea of socializing was having a glass of Babycham once a year with the next door neighbour, who incidentally was a female widow. Ok there was my dad, but frankly he didn't stand a chance in terms of male assertion and as he worked shifts we didn't see that much of him anyway. All this, coupled with the fact of me having ever such a sensitive artistic nature (alright then, I was awkward and shy), meant that I battled with the ability to perceive boys as being remotely approachable; after all they were from a different planet and existed in a parallel universe to mine...... Yes, well alright people can change.

Anyway, the fact is that in my eyes, it was less a question of blokes being from Mars, but more one of them not even being in the same stratosphere.

Obviously a lot of water has passed under the bridge since then. Despite the fact that I can no longer really be deemed as being shy or introverted and despite the fact that I am now prepared to acknowledge that the male species are, on the whole, part of the same race as myself, I do still occasionally revert back to those early days of gaucheness.

I partly blame this on the fact that art societies appear to be mainly comprised of women that are on the whole, heading towards (myself included), or have arrived at, that time of one's cycle that is generally regarded as the 'twilight zone'. So you can imagine the effect on me when I very occasionally find myself in a situation where there is a token male or two in the room, and if the said male is under the age of eighty-five (another rarity), and doesn't look like he's been run over by a bus, it completely throws me. This is where I find myself getting all self-conscious and 'girly', which is tragic enough, considering I am over sixty, but also that I suddenly start to suffer from 'empty head' syndrome, which is not great if you are trying to deliver a talk.

I don't even have to fancy the impostor, but just catching sight of that manly countenance in amongst the 'coven' is enough to throw me. I usually manage to pull myself together afterwards, as I go round the group individually to advise them on their work, when I discover that the Adonis is a know-it-all, with nasal hair and a Brummie accent, whereby I revert to type and start bossing him around like I do the others.

In my experience, there is another thing that you must avoid at all costs if you want to maintain any semblance of credibility as a professional tutor who wants to give the illusion of knowing what they are doing; this is 'the demonstration'.

Don't be fooled into convincing yourself that you can pull it off. Take it from one who knows, that the paint will run where you don't want it to and half way through you will discover that you've forgotten to bring along that vital piece of equipment.....your brain.

Initially you feel quite encouraged, as you become mesmerized by the rapt anticipation on the faces of your captive audience. It's only when you start to get the thing underway, that you wake up and realise that the little scenario that you have just witnessed, the one where you pull-off a successful painting, was in fact a fantasy in your head, and the panic starts to set in when you acknowledge the fact that you've bitten off more than you can chew.

It isn't like I don't know my subject. It's just that performing like a monkey in front of an audience, under the restraint of a very limited time factor, is not a natural situation in which to be creative. I can't think of many occasions where you would come out on top, after doing a party trick in twenty minutes, a task that would normally take you two days to perform. I suppose I might be persuaded to try a bit harder if I were being paid vast amounts of money on television, but we're talking about a workshop in a village hall here.

Anyway, you have a choice when you find yourself in this kind of situation. If you have stupidly got yourself into this mess, you can either brazen it out, or admit that you can't possibly make whatever you are doing work under the circumstances. You must always choose option one. If you go down the honest road, the group will look at you scornfully and exchange nods with one another that show they are fully aware that you are in fact a numskull, a charlatan, that is posing as an expert. No, the braying hounds want blood for their money – the show must go on. Much better to make a spectacle of yourself confidently and with panache. That way your audience will start to question their own critical judgement and you will get away with the fact that what you have produced, is in fact, trash. Bit like the 'Emperor's New Clothes'. You could tell them in great depth, how you've just swept the floor or had a fried egg for breakfast – do it with enough confidence and a flourish and they'll find it riveting.

*   *   *

The various subject matters that I have taught, under the umbrella of Art, have been widely varied over the years; portraits, landscape, interiors, cottages to name but a few, but the discipline that has proved to be the most controversial is Life Drawing.

The general reaction from civilians, when you tell them that you teach this subject, is invariably as follows: "What you mean nude.....naked.....undressed, starkers, what nothing on at all"? It's amazing how many different ways there are to say 'sans kit'. This is of course always accompanied by sniggering and nudging, and usually the conversation continues along the lines of "Eh, our Fred'll do it for you love; Fred, she wants you to be a nude model …… go on …….he'll pose for you, won't you Fred? Go on, he'll get is togs off." Then more snorting and wiping of eyes, followed by "Eh Jasmine, your dad's going to be a model". "Oh yer, go on dad, it'll be a right laugh" (who for?) This little conversation can be quite a crowd puller.

It's no good me getting all holier-than-thou and saying "but it's a job", or explaining how beneficial and essential it is for art students to draw the human figure, they just laugh more and nod knowingly. Their opinion of me, tends to either go up or down in their estimation, depending on their predilection towards perversion. Either way it ain't good!

I was recently asked by an art society to give them their first ever life drawing session. This workshop was to take place in a yacht club in a small, fairly posh sea-side resort close to where I live. I made all the necessary arrangements, making sure the room would be adequately heated and the windows covered, so as not to be overlooked by any would-be gawpers, and I had booked a lovely professional model. Two days before the big day I received a phone-call, informing me that the 'brown owl' or whatever those people are called that run yacht clubs, although not a member of the art group herself, had forbidden the class to take place, because she felt this subject would be too licentious for the residents of this salubrious resort to cope with. Heavens! How did she imagine Rubens or for that matter any of the hundreds of great artists throughout the history of art coped ..... and what about all those religious iconic paintings with nude cherubs dripping gold all over the place ...... shocking! Presumably she saw any art form depicting the nude as a licence for debauchery – personally I felt it said more about her mind than anyone else's. But the day was saved in the end as I told the model simply to keep her clothes on. Life under wraps.

Having experienced life drawing for many years, both in a doing and teaching capacity, I have, I suppose, become a bit blasé about the whole idea of nudity. That's not to say that I fancy having a go myself, (I can't reconcile myself to the idea of sitting on chairs where several other naked bums have perched), and I wouldn't like to scar my students for life, but I am not easily shocked.

Models come in all shapes and sizes, but ultimately are, after all, of the same species as ourselves (although there have been one or two occasions over the years when I've wondered). It is the very nature of this fact, that makes it such a difficult and exacting type of drawing to do, and therefore such a valuable discipline for artists to experience. When we look at a drawing of the human figure, in a sense we are looking at ourselves. We know exactly where all the bits and bobs are meant to go and can tell instantly if something is a bit out. You don't have to be a slave to the mirror to be an expert in recognizing more or less how we should look, because we see ourselves everyday. Move a branch on a tree and no-one will be any the wiser, but place an arm slightly off course and you've had it, so unlike other subjects you can't cheat or get away with slapdash draughtsmanship or stylized mark-making (unless your name is Picasso) if you want your rendition of the model to look anything like a human being.

I believe that modelling is an incredibly underestimated job. It is common for anyone that's never tried it to say things like "that must be money for old rope, just laying/sitting there all day. In reality, it can be physically gruelling, having to stay in any position (no matter how comfortable it feels to start with), for any length of time. Then of course there are the imaginary itches that invade every cell in your brain when you know you aren't meant to move, not to mention the fact that everyone else in the room is clothed and you are starkers.

Being drawn by anyone, let alone a group of students

that are learning and making mistakes, means that the model needs to possess immense forbearing and strength of character when they find themselves confronted at the end of a session with an assortment of drawings that would shock the special effects team for the Rocky Horror show.

I have on the odd occasion, sat for half an hour or so (clothed) if the model has not turned up. The first time I did this I had a nasty shock when I came to view the pictures afterwards, and discovered that I had not been depicted as the attractive, young looking person that I had been deluding myself into thinking I was all these years, but that my little sunflowers saw me as a lumpy old bag with a turned up nose and several chins. I was tempted to throw myself under the next bus, but as I live in the sticks this wasn't due for another four hours by which time I'd calmed down. If ever I find myself in this situation now, I get round the problem by reminding them that I will be assessing them at the end of term so it might be an idea to employ a bit of artistic licence.

From a teaching aspect it can be difficult keeping a large group of students stimulated/motivated/under control, whilst at the same time making sure that whoever is modelling hasn't flaked out, as has happened on three occasions. It's always reassuring when you hear the tell-tale snort that tells you they are merely sleeping and haven't actually passed out, or even away, whilst they have been posing.

I have always prided myself on my consideration for models; not making them hang upside-down from the light-fittings and making sure they have lots of breaks etc. One model I used several years ago took advantage of my kindness by accusing me of being unreasonable if I asked her to keep still for longer than ten minutes.

I admit, I have…. erm….. once or twice been known to forget, in my enthusiasm to extract small miracles from the students, that a model has been in one position for long enough to start developing pressure sores. I was presented one Christmas with a small package from one such unlucky muse, and was quite frankly touched that she had obviously forgiven me enough to buy me a festive gift, only to find upon opening it, an alarm clock with a digital seconds button. The fact that it was in the guise of a pink plastic cow may or may not have been significant. Esmerelda has been a constant companion ever since, apart from the time when a group of students kidnapped her and I had to place 'has anyone seen my cow' posters around the college, until she was found in the bottom of the vice principal's stationery cupboard.

As I have said, life drawing is not an easy thing to contend with. The room often has to be heated to tropical levels (depending on the hardiness of the model). Students can grind away for hours, only to find that the head of the unfortunate subject would be better placed on the shoulders of a leprechaun rather than an average sized person; either that or they finish up with a bad case of hydrocephalus.

Sometimes when I am teaching I find it easier and more appropriate to show a student how to correct something by demonstrating on their actual drawing, rather than trying to verbally explain. I have to be careful not to get carried away at such times and have been known get a bit possessive. I was recently pulled up sharp when a girl that I was helping stood by patiently, well yes ok, for quite a while actually, before she timidly said "can I have a little go now". Occasionally it can come to fisticuffs when I have been known to wrestle over a piece of charcoal. Anyway, no doubt I'll get the sack after this so it won't matter one way or the other.

Hands invariably prove to be problematic when drawing the figure. I was helping someone several years ago during an evening class, when she snapped that I had given the model six fingers. Well ok there was the extra one, but what she had failed to notice is that it was beautifully drawn. Well, you can't have everything can you. I've seen 'em all over the years, every denotation of the human hand (and some that might well have been derived from other life forms); the talons, the mittens, the rubber glove syndrome, the mutants.

Some students think they can outsmart me by deliberately doing their drawing so big that they conveniently don't have room to fit the hands and feet on the page. I now keep what I call 'the bits jar' in my teaching room, especially for this little ruse, whereby anyone leaving off any extremities like the head, mitts or piggies, has to put money in the jar; its currently 5p per hand or foot, 10p for a whole leg or arm, and 30p for a head. This is actually my retirement fund but the trouble is the little buggers are getting wise to me now, so at this rate I'll still be working when I'm ninety.

I have toughened up regarding the potential problem of being embarrassed at the prospect of coming face-to-face (or whatever) with a naked person. In fact I sometimes forget when I'm setting up a pose; like the time when I got a male model to sit backwards astride one of those plastic bucket type chairs with the hole in the back. Do I need to spell out the intricacies of the unfortunate alignment my positioning had thrown up, or should I say out! But I am always ever so professional I wouldn't dream of giggling inappropriately.

I once found myself in the rather uncomfortable position of using a friend as a model. At the time I was in need of a male model (this isn't what it seems), and a friend of mine got so fed up hearing me blathering on about how hard it is to get anyone to do the job, that he offered himself up as a sacrifice. After enduring the epic length application forms and police checks (to be honest I've always felt that the models needed more protection from the students than the other way round), he was ready to face the music.

What had seemed like a great idea whilst in a drunken stupor in the pub, suddenly became an excruciatingly embarrassing situation. The poor bloke, lets call him John, was so mortified on his first day, that his embarrassment was contagious and even I, who had been previously impervious to such sensibilities, found myself with very rosy cheeks when it came to the showdown. The students of course picked up on this and spent the morning tittering. The fruits of this first session amounted to lots of back views. During the week John asked tentatively if it would be alright for him to wear a thong in future, which I heartily agreed to. I am not fibbing when I tell you that he appeared at the next session sporting a silver look thong which he had purchased from ……. Wait for it …… Peacocks. He has forever since been known as 'John the thong', having been unsuccessful in begging me to keep my mouth shut. I hadn't realised Peacocks ran to such things and wondered if their fashion buyer was aiming for the man on the street's version of Anne Summers.

I had a very enthusiastic model a couple of years ago. As it was the beginning of term and still only September and the weather was glorious, I decided to take pity on my students and suggested that we de-camp outside to do some clothed poses in the college grounds.

This man is a keen golfer and as he had his equipment in the back of his car, I suggested some pretend action poses of him practicing his swipe or whatever. All went well until Alan's need to prove his golfing prowess got the better of him, and instead of going through the motions of hitting the ball, he went the whole hog and actually hit it. He gave it such a wallop that it crossed the recreational area, narrowly missing several innocent bystanders, before landing with a bang against the side of a rather expensive looking car, where it ricocheted off and hit the window with a bang, before dropping to the ground and rolling with a flourish across the car park. Like in a car crash, I witnessed in slow motion the twenty-six O shapes of the student's mouths on that afternoon, before I ran and hid behind a large nearby tree. I had an older student in the group at that time so my thinking was that if I disappeared, any irate witnesses would assume that she was the tutor and she could take the rap. Approximately five minutes later, the caretaker (whose bad books I was still in after an incident involving blocked drains and acrylic paint), accompanied by presumably the owner of the car, strolled casually out of the building, walked casually around the car ..... three times, then strolled casually back into the building. Five minutes later I came out of hiding, strolled casually over to the scene of the crime, strolled casually around the car..... three times, before casually strolling back to my tree.

I'm pretty certain that there was more than a bit of divine intervention at play on that day because there was not a scratch, mark or bump to be found on the car. Alan however, was heard to tell people during the following week, that he had walked into a lamppost.

One female model I had once asked if she could bring her new baby into college as she was still feeding her. I thought this might prove to be an interesting experience for the students to draw her and the wee one, as indeed to start with it was. We carried the sweet little sleeping baby in it's carry-cot to the life drawing studio where there was lots of ahs and cooing, and I felt proud to be providing such innovative subject matter for my students to draw... until ... the Kraken awoke. The angelic chrysalis had hatched into a pink monster. The rest of the day was one long round of screaming (me and the baby), disappearing into the cupboard that served as the model's changing room (literally in this case), feeding, winding, two minutes drawing, more screaming, then finally ending on a high note when it threw up all over a freshly washed throw, before I begged her to take the thing away; most of the boys had already left by this time, which is interesting and just goes to prove that they don't have as much stamina as girls.

I once made the big mistake of placing some ads in various shop windows to advertise for a model. It was around this time that the funny phone calls started. The ones that I remember most were from a bloke called Dave. Dave phoned regular as clockwork every Thursday evening between 5 – 7pm for a period of approximately two months (presumably when his wife was attending her yoga class), and as the telly was rubbish, I decided to humour him.

To start with there was the usual laughing (on his part) and the drunken promises: "I promise you darlin, I'm just what you're looking for/need" etc. etc. I went through the motions each week of relaying my usual response to this kind of thing, by telling him to fuck off and get a life, but I have to say I'd begun to admire his perseverance, well yes, he did have real staying power. Then after a few weeks he began to tell me that actually he was only phoning for a laugh and that he wasn't really serious about modeling at all. No! really?

Phase three consisted of him telling me that he'd been made redundant and so had a bit of time on his hands and his wife was doing her best (I can imagine), and one of his kids had gone off the rails, and actually I began to feel a bit sorry for the poor sod. I was just starting to think that I might have missed my vocation and that perhaps I should re train to become a Relate officer or offer my services to the Samaritans, when the phone calls abruptly stopped. I like to think it was because he'd landed a new job.

*   *   *

A few years ago I decided it was time to cut my hours down at the college where I teach, when I found myself having more and more arguments with the students and staff …… in my kitchen …… at home ….. on my own.

The really great thing about this of course, is that no-one answers you back, the downside is that it means you are going insane. Don't get me wrong, I've always talked to myself, but these rows were becoming so impassioned that I was becoming in danger of having to ask myself to keep the noise down. I was aware that I was tripping merrily along a very slippery slope.

Another determining factor in my decision, was when the art technician came into the staff room one day and said "last year again is it Wend"? This after the annual row with my boss that occurred at the end of every academic year and resulted in me storming out and saying "that's it! I'm never coming back to this bloody place again". Even I was sick of hearing myself say those words.

I do such a small amount of teaching at this establishment now that there is very little time for any shenanigans and we all walk around smiling nicely at each other (yuk!) .... until that is, the end of year show. Try to imagine this in quivering letters, dripping blood if you can. This is the time when the painted smiles and sickly politeness are quickly replaced by a year's worth of pent up snarling, bitching, swearing and shouting, that we've all somehow managed to keep in check.

Now, in theory, putting up a show of the fruits of a couple of year's hard labour should be a joyous opportunity to showcase the student's work ...... I hesitate here because it's actually quite hard to convey mirthless laughter in written form, but try to imagine it if you can.

This great event usually entails me and another couple of hapless staff, arguing about which pieces to put where (don't tempt me) in an unrealistically short space of time, whilst the students, in the early stages of this extravaganza, are generally arsing around and showing not the least bit of interest in their own work, despite us screaming at them to join in.

After the first day something happens, whereupon the little darlings suddenly turn into the most theatrical, outrageous prima-donnas and drama queens, as the reality sinks in, that yes, this is their show, and yes, their loved ones will soon be seeing just what they've been investing their hard-earned readies in over the last few years.

The ensuing day and a half consists of students having mini-breakdowns and staff having major ones, bodies huddled in corners having nosebleeds, crying episodes so severe that the work is in danger of running, tantrums, theatrical sobbing, outbursts of "I hate all my work", "I hate you", "I don't want that piece up", "I've lost that project", "I've lost all my work", "there's no more sticky tabs" …….. on and on …. Well, I suppose they are in training to become artists.

Anyway, it stands to reason that someone has to

stand firm ……..

I felt quite flattered that I always seemed to be dragged in to help organize this event, thinking my aesthetic and artistic skills were much appreciated and even depended upon, until I realised with a cold shock one day that I was being enlisted for other qualities, when my boss said admiringly "you turn into a Dictator at this time of year Wendy". No-one wants to be compared to Bill Sykes, and sadly I began to wonder if I should trade my sheepdog in for a pit-bull terrier.

Miraculously though, everything seems to come together, and by the time of the preview, most people are actually on speaking terms again. Although come to think of it, there was that year when I got so hysterical with a group of naughty students, that my shouting was heard up two flights of stairs and there was a lot of pointing out, withering looks and "look that's' her" and "there's that cow" at the event.

One year I got so fed up with all the histrionics that I decided to have a few of my own by walking out in the middle of putting the show up and popping into town for an impromptu hairdo with my very accommodating hairdresser. She even let me have a go with her stress ball, that she kept in for when she had to cope with difficult customers like me. I felt so much better afterwards and had lots of lovely compliments about my hair at the opening.

*   *   *

While I'm on a roll, I'd just like to give a tiny mention to paperwork, which has of course now gone beyond all reason. In fact the whole subject of filling out form after form, trying to stuff something which is essentially creative into little boxes, and attempting to find seven different ways to say the same thing, has become such a bore that I can't even be bothered to think about it. I'm tired of hearing us all going on (myself more than most) about the ridiculous ways that we have to justify receiving a meager wage at the end of each month.

My paperwork at college is nothing compared to what the full-time staff have to contend with, yet it has quadrupled compared to what it was when I first started teaching there seventeen years ago. But does this make any difference to the quality of teaching .... Yes, of course, it means that staff have much less time now to teach.

Each year a new piece of paper is brought out and added to the existing pile, the content of which you need a PhD to understand. I have been teaching for over twenty-five years; I have a Degree, I have an excellent track record (if you ignore the death, the shouting and the violence), and I have proved myself as a teacher and an expert in my field. Yet despite my experience, I am on a lower rate of pay than someone coming into the profession newly graduated from college, because I don't have a piece of paper that says I can teach.

I wonder what would happen if Richard Branson were to offer to run a course in business studies: "Yes Rich, we'd be delighted to have you on board, but you'll be on the unqualified rate of pay because you haven't got a PGCE".

I'm not saying that people in any situation shouldn't be accountable or be assessed periodically. Let's face it the Miss Jones's of the world could have done with a bit of regulation, but most people I know would agree that we've taken things too far.

Although I only teach part-time, I take my role in playing a part in the development of students seriously and am dedicated to passing on as much knowledge as I am able, but I have to say that when it comes to the end of term paperwork, the only way I can prevent myself from losing the will to live is by tackling it after a large glass of wine (or two) in the evening. The upshot of this, what with the alcohol, the fact that it is past 10pm, and the pointless tedium of the task, is that I invariably nod off at regular intervals, with my pen poised ready for action over the forms, resulting in a curious series of shorthand-like squiggles on the paper as my hand is being guided, presumably by some spirit or other, over the paper. It is interesting, and shows I think, a serious level of commitment on my part, that I am able to maintain my duties even when I am unconscious. I did have a bit of an uncomfortable moment recently when handing in my assessment forms, when my boss said "Wendy, why are there always those funny marks all over the pages"? I laughingly told him that my naughty (imaginary) cat likes to walk over the table when I am working. There we go, another reason to sack me.

A colleague and I tried to inject a bit of interest into written work a few years ago, by making up words to slip in; this little ruse can also liven up meetings by the way. As we have never been picked up on our naughtiness, I can only assume that the stuff is never read and that we are never listened to.

It is surprising really isn't it? the different ways people can try to disguise 'dullness' in an attempt to alleviate potential boredom. One of the workshops that I have devised as part of my subject repertoire for teaching is called 'Making a Silk Purse out of a Sow's Ear'. This consists of me taking along a bag full of dishwater-dreary photographs (taken by me), tipping them out on a table, and telling the group to "make something glorious from them". Believe it or not this actually works because it means that they have to use a considerable amount of imagination and artistic license in order to produce anything remotely interesting from such boring dross.

I have on occasions been in situations where I have been enthusiastically clapped after delivering particularly long talks; you know, the kind where you can see out of the corner of your eye, people doing good impressions of those dogs with the nodding heads that were popular in the seventies. I've a sneaking suspicion that the ensuing applause may have less to do with the quality of my lecture, but more to do with the fact that I have finally stopped talking ..... yeeeees, she's stopped!

*   *   *

I have of course, during my years spent training to become a 'country bumpkin' and offering myself up as a sacrifice to the world of teaching, been continuing on my journey as a painter, which was really the main reason, apart from fearing the loss of my sanity, I wanted to cut my teaching hours down. This journey has been, and continues to be a struggle. Just as you start to feel that you are beginning to get somewhere, the goalposts move again. Anyway, I've come to accept that it will more than probably always be that way. Like in the words of the old Chinese proverb 'Foolish man say – "Hey! I think I've cracked it", Confucius say, "No my friend, your work's still shit".

Every so often though, there is a little break in the clouds and the Sun shows through just long enough for you to be temporarily deluded into thinking that you are getting somewhere.

Being naturally shy, retiring and modest, it does not come easily for me to share any bit of success I may have encountered on my journey. What?

Several years ago I entered quite a prestigious landscape painting competition, won the regional prize for Wales and was runner-up for the National prize for Britain. This went completely to my head and I entered the competition again a couple of years later.

Following a horrendous train journey to London that encompassed major engineering works on the line, a bus shuttle service in operation between stations and a cramped train with a grumpy old guard who informed me that "next time you'll av to pay for em", referring to the two rather large paintings that I'd been wrestling with during this debacle, I managed against all the odds to deliver my submission for the competition in the nick of time to meet the deadline, before embarking on the nightmare journey home in reverse (albeit minus the paintings).

There is obviously something in the old adage 'no pain no gain' because three days later I was informed that I had won first prize in the competition.

I actually went on to win this competition again (whoops sorry, just adjusting my head band) a few years later, before the company that sponsored it disappeared, undoing the notion of certain 'friends' that the first win must have been a fluke.

My theory regarding the demise of these generous patrons is that if they were investing as much in their 'works do's' as they were in the sponsorship of the arts, then I'm not surprised that they eventually went down the pan.

Winners, along with their partners, were put up in a posh hotel in London for a night, then ferried by taxi to a champagne reception held at the Mall Galleries. It was really gorgeous and we were treated like celebrities, (well in my eyes anyway ….. remember I don't get out much).

By this time, the relationship with my Welshman was beginning to show a few cracks, plus someone had to look after the dog, which resulted in me being accompanied to the event by my long-suffering sister Susan who had finally forgiven me for the Brighton fiasco (although I feel that some of her magnanimousness may have been more to do with the prospect of a free night out).

We were both so nervous on our arrival for the prize-giving ceremony that we downed the constant stream of champagne that was thrust at us, like it was cream soda, so by the time of the actual dishing out of the prizes I could barely stand up and Susan, having deposited her quails eggs in a nearby pot plant, had disappeared. I've a rather fetching photograph somewhere or other of me 'listing to starboard' against the Chairman of the company as he handed me the winner's cheque. We later managed to sit through a dinner back at the hotel with some of the other artists, but they were all pissed too so we didn't feel out of place.

I admit that I am rather embarrassed now when I think back to my lack of sophistication, hell no, let's be honest, my total lack of any semblance of adult, respectable behaviour, but I suppose it will always be a memorable occasion.

On my entry into the fray on my successive win two years later, I was manhandled rather forcefully I thought, by the nice Irish lady who was still organizing the event, who after warmly congratulating me, suggested that I might want to ease off the sauce this time.

I did go on to have some further success with various competitions which was great, except I was beginning to realise that winning was becoming more important than doing the painting. I'd also of course noticed that I wasn't actually winning anything anymore, plus it was getting a bit expensive to enter.

The other thing that you have to cope with in this sort of situation is the 'fall-out' after any success. Initially well-meaning friends tell you "oh well, this is it, you'll be made now", and "it's a turning point" and "it's your round". Ha, don't believe a word of it. What actually happens, is that when the excitement of seeing the ghastly photo of you pointing at some blurred makeshift picture that you've whipped off the wall and placed on your easel, with your accompanying miss-spelt name, has diminished, you are left to settle back down into oblivion again, which is exactly how things were before you entered the competition; a bit like your blood-sugar level after a chocolate fix.

As I have already hinted, the relationship with Mihangel was by this time going firmly off the rails. We had enjoyed five great years of long-distance romance, before making the more permanent commitment of living together. After a few years of him maintaining his job in Kent and commuting home to Wales at the weekends, he eventually took early retirement, resulting in two over-sensitive, emotional artists living under the same roof …. 24hrs a day. This wasn't always easy, but we did have lots of good times. However, after ten years of co-habiting, I realised with a bit of a shock one day, that I didn't know who I was. I don't mean that I'd received a blow to the head, and I realise this must sound a bit strange, but I had never really had a time when I'd got to know me properly. There had been those wonderful self-indulgent years at art college, but that was a very intense and focused time, so not really a great opportunity to contemplate more esoteric matters.

Between having gone through a difficult childhood

and co-habiting with someone virtually all my adult life, I felt that I had always been in a situation where other's needs had taken precedence over my own. In my adult relationships this was of course my own fault, as I am by nature a true martyr, and instead of actually standing up and saying no to situations that were not right for me, I allowed myself to be swept along in the tide of someone else's wake. Anyway, things came to a head after ten years of living together and we finally untied our apron strings.

Although it was very difficult at first to adjust to our new situations, we both decided, after a period of blaming/hating/shouting at each other, that actually, we did still like/love and respect one another enough to want to remain friends.

My relationship with this man has been character-building in the best possible sense. I have benefited from and been influenced by his wisdom, humour and intelligence, and remain the very best of friends with both him and his lovely wife Ceri, who along with a few other close friends, prop me up when I'm going through yet another crisis.

ON THE EDGE

Wendy Murphy

One of the most significant changes to my life since becoming an artist has been my image. This encompasses not only my own perception of myself, but that of other people's too; or more to the point other people's expectations of what they imagine the life of an artist to be.

The idea of us arty lot being a load of brainless bohemians really became fashionable with the increasing emphasis on the importance of all things technological. Oh I know that we all do it. I am just as guilty of stereotyping other groups of people in society. When I think of a banker or an accountant, I immediately, and no doubt unfairly, think of the colour 'grey', but perhaps this is to do with the fact that given my general state of poverty, these people don't feature big in my life.

I am of course generalizing here. I know that lots of people, if they think of us at all, don't see artists as anything other than slightly strange folk that spend their lives beavering away creating stuff for reasons known only to themselves. Although, thinking about it, I don't know either why I do what I do – but it's certainly not for financial reward.

In my experience, I have encountered many people that have been encouraging and supportive and I've received some lovely compliments about my work over the years. There is undoubtedly though, still a chunk of the population who judging from some of the comments that I have heard, see artists as daubers that don't warrant a place on the professional ladder.

The upside of being 'cut loose' as it were, from the confines of the 'professional club' these days, is that we do at least have the freedom to express ourselves without feeling under pressure to pander to the vanities of a rich patron; (chance would be a fine thing).

The interesting thing is though, as far as I can see, there is a turning point when the fickle surveyor of art will drastically turn about face from having this negative attitude towards artists, to suddenly 'seeing the light' of recognition and appreciation at the first sniff of fame. Today Paul is a scruffy dreamer, going under the title of 'artist', but the mere mention of his being on TV or the radio, talking about his work, either that or the fact that he has just died, renders him a genius and the greatest living artist of this century. I have lost count of the number of greatest living artist ever's there have been.

Personally, I studied for five years, my ex partner for seven. Yet in comparison to other professionals studying and working in a variety of fields, the artist can receive very different treatment and is often not taken seriously; You can almost hear what they're thinking, 'oh, a Degree in art, that doesn't really count does it'.

The idea of art as a subject being seen as 'a soft option' is very prevalent still. We do get a certain amount of students that join the courses in college in

September, that are under the illusion that doing art will be a doddle – they have usually left the course by Christmas. Parents too, can sometimes fall into the trap of shoving their offspring into Art simply because they don't appear to be much good for anything else, and they must be seen to be going on into further education whether they are suited to it or not. Still, I suppose it does keep them off the streets, and helps to keep the unemployment figures down, even if it's not really a serious profession.

Mihangel and his father, (a qualified electrician that had reached the top of his profession) were estranged for a number of years, because like my own father, he could not reconcile himself to the fact that his son had not chosen, in his eyes, a more respectable career. When he eventually heard that Mihangel was head of a Degree course and had been lecturing for several years, he said "I hear you've got a 'proper job' at last" and promptly welcomed him back into the fold.

I can understand that parents might feel concerned that their offspring may be entering into a profession where they will be struggling, in all senses of the word, but I'm pretty sure that resistance doesn't always stem from such noble misgivings.

It's a nuisance really, as I'm enjoying feeling all self-righteous, persecuted and misunderstood, that there is always some well meaning civilian to come along and spoil my martyrdom by being nice to me.

113

It's annoying, but I have to admit, I have met some truly lovely civilians during my time as a painter. There are lots of people around that although Art might not be 'their thing', are still willing to at least acknowledge that I am actually working, even if it isn't in a 9-5 job with a regular salary at the end of each month; and to recognise that I am in a profession which is precarious to say the least, when it comes to earning a living.

I have had more offers of kindness when I have been particularly down on my uppers than I would ever imagine I would need or get. Oh, but it's so much more enjoyable talking about the naughty civilians than it is the goodies, so let me have my fun.

I suppose part of the reason that I seem to have developed a somewhat jaundiced view of those members of the public that do lack understanding or appreciation of what an artist does, stems from the fact that because I sell in the main through galleries, I don't often get to meet the people who genuinely love art, so I finish up hearing the views of those that may not have a great interest in painting so put forward uninformed views of the subject. I suppose I'm a bit like a Dr. that gets to mainly see sick people. Oh Lord! That came out all wrong, but you get the gist.

My paintings more often than not, are born after a fairly difficult birth – so when they are finally ready to make their way, out in the big competitive world, jostling for space along with other pictures on a gallery wall, it can feel a bit like I imagine it must be when your offspring leaves home for the first time.

I must admit, when I first started out in the business, I felt the loss of those early paintings that I sold, much more keenly than I do now, whereby my need to eat seems to have taken over and made me much less precious; nevertheless, I do still like to think of my pictures having gone to good homes. It's a strange feeling to think that there are little bits of me in other people's homes all over Britain.

In some instances, people that like your work can buy several pieces, sometimes over a period of years. Occasionally I have met them, either at previews or at home, and on these occasions I have had my faith in human nature restored, as they generally turn out to be charming, and I find myself having to eat my acerbic words to such an extent, that I finish up with a bad case of acid indigestion.

I certainly don't expect everyone to like what I do and I am not suggesting that everyone should rush out and enrol on an Art appreciation course. I accept that we all have different strengths and interests – I just don't want to be told that my work is overpriced, that it doesn't look like it's taken very long, or that I am not really working, by someone that may know very little about me, painting, or what it is like to be an artist.

I have to admit that when I meet someone for the first

time and they ask me what I do for a living, when I tell them I am a painter, I do often quickly follow this up by informing them that I am also a part-time lecturer in order to award myself more credibility. I really must stop doing that!

With regard to my career, I would say that I'm at the 'rinse-hold' stage of my artistic cycle.

Doing some research recently into various art galleries, I realized that the average age of the artists that had 'made it' in terms of recognition and respect, was between 64-92yrs, which gave me a bit of hope, that despite the fact that time does seem to be speeding up, and well, let's face it, running out, I may still be in with a chance of moving on to the 'fast spin' of success stage.

You may be forgiven for thinking that as a creative person, I should be above mentioning such earthly delights as success, but I am also a human being, and despite being dedicated to the ongoing need to achieve excellence as a painter, there is still a part of me that would dearly like to show off a bit. Oh, and I also need to eat, so I wouldn't say no to a bit of remunerative compensation. I am not daubing all artists with the same brush as myself, and I am certainly no less dedicated to my cause, but be aware that some of us do still have egos.

*　　*　　*

In the meantime, I have to confess that mostly I am only too happy to oblige those people that are still hanging on to the clichéd perception of the arty image. It gives me a wonderful excuse to be a hedonistic slut, with grubby fingernails, crumpled clothes and a tendency to have long conversations with myself. Is it any wonder I live alone?

However, there are odd times when I get heartily sick of this persona and it is during these little absences that I yearn for the regimented normality of the luncheon voucher years, not to mention the regular pay slips at the end of each month. Whilst experiencing these delusional moments I stupidly imagine that I can slip through the back of the art cupboard and pretend that, actually, I am really a perfectly 'normal' person after all. Ha ha.

If after a few days I haven't tired of wearing colour co-ordinated clothes, scrubbing my fingernails of the last vestiges of paint, and closing the door of my studio in an attempt to hide the smell of turps, I usually find that I can count on someone else to expose me for cranky slattern that I seem to have become.

More often than not, I can rely on my friend's husband to step in and remind me, not to mention the neighbours, that I will never be one of them.

Let me tell you that Robin and his wife Lavinia, (I was going to change their names in case they decided to pay me back by suing me, after the losing our lunch down the ravine incident, but they have assured me that it's all water under the bridge now), are a wee bit on the eccentric side. I'm sorry, but anyone that has a drawbridge going up to their front door and is currently building a 'Greek temple' made out of railway sleepers in the back garden, has to be a little odd, and well, yes, they are, coincidentally, both artists.

Now remember that I live in a very small community, where all the locals know your darkest secret (even if it is only a passion for liquorice) what you had for dinner last night, but more importantly, who your friends are. When I tell you that Robin has a penchant for 'dummies' and makes no attempt to hide his fetish, you will start to realize that the sheer fact that I am known to be very good friends with these people, makes it impossible for me to get away with hiding behind the façade of being perfectly 'normal'. Through no fault of my own, and in the words of Lizzy Bennet in 'Pride and Prejudice', "I am tainted by association".

Judas-like, I have tried denying the friendship by only visiting their house after dark in a long coat with a hood and dark glasses, but that only serves to fuel the conviction of whoever I am inevitably spotted by, that I too, am indeed, very odd.

I am aware that I have left you in limbo a bit over the mention of 'dummies' so would just like to stress that I am not referring to sucky dum-dums here, but rather, the type to be found in shop windows, or as Robin likes to huffily correct me , "mannequins, they're mannequins Wendy, don't keep calling them dummies"…. yea, whatever, as if that makes it any better. I would also like, at this point, to tell you quite categorically, that I am in no way party to any shifty or perverse goings on that locals may have heard about, and anyway that business involving the mechanical digger was sorted out in the end.

I don't quite know how to say this, but there are to date ……. well ……. twenty- two dummies residing at this residence (my friends have a big house). Most of the 'girls' are imprisoned in the garage, various sheds, and one dusky maiden is I believe in the coal bunker, but the four favourites are proudly ensconced in the house.

I'd always believed (or perhaps I needed to believe) that Lavinia had been an innocent victim in all this and I felt very sorry that she had had to share her home all these years, not to mention her husband, with the 'resin rivals', until I overheard her one day suggesting it was time to change 'Marigold's' jewellery.

The four 'chosen ones' are very lucky girls indeed. Not only are they, unlike many of the unfortunate amputees outside, of sound limb, but they are also (apart from the slutty one in the TV room) very tastefully dressed and bedecked in some rather fine jewellery.

I had been caught on several occasions eyeing them up enviously, until Robin said nastily one day, when he caught me drooling over Diana's necklace, "forget it love, we've done an inventory". Pervert!

Actually, I've just had a little thought, I wonder if I ever find myself homeless …….you can see what I'm thinking here ……

I did once try to 'cure' Robin of, what I on more compassionate days refer to as his illness, by placing Marigold in the marital bed when I was looking after their house while they were on holiday, thinking it would give him a bit of a turn when they came home. Pity really that I wasn't there to witness the impact, because apparently he was heard to scream upon entering the bedroom…… and yet…. still ….. he persists in his strange ways, and I sadly, am still tarred with the brush of peculiarity.

I suppose if I am honest, as a breed we artists don't exactly help ourselves when it comes to establishing ourselves on the 'normality scale'.

My ex partner Mihangel and his wife Ceri live in the aforementioned rustic Elizabethan farmhouse ……. complete with year round flashing Christmas lights and decorations …….. inside and out. Ceri is not even an artist, yet she has sadly become an innocent casualty as a result of living with one. She has now, I'm afraid, gone over to the dark side altogether. I realized this, with a heavy heart one day, when I spotted her at a preview sporting a papier-mâché peacock complete with sequins and feathers on the shoulder of her outfit (which come to think of it I bought her).

Mihangel is currently delving into the art of bookbinding and has enlisted the help of his friends by ordering them to save any potentially suitable materials (usually this means anything unsavoury) that can be used for the preparation of the covers. I didn't mind gathering oak apples that can be ground down for the tannin, or even seaweed but I did start to get a bit fed up when I was constantly being nagged to save my fish skins.

My continuing apprehension and concern regarding the welfare of his wife was compounded one day when I visited their home and she nonchalantly said "come and sit here my dear ….. by the pork". I am not talking hot sizzling crackling clad dinner here, but rather, lumps of raw pig skin plastered with salt and still sporting the occasional bristle, hanging like a canopy from the ceiling over the fire. As I picked my way through various groceries that were scattered over chairs, tables and the floor, she met my puzzled frown by casually telling me that they'd had an ASDA delivery that day but had nowhere to put the shopping as the fridge was full of road-kill.

My own image of course, is really rather pedestrian in comparison. I've never quite managed to shake off my indoctrination into civilian life, so am caught in a kind of purgatory somewhere in between the two worlds. If you ignore the talking-to-myself, (well loads of people do that don't they?) I don't see that having a stuffed sable called Wilfred, draped along the back of my sofa, necessarily means that I am odd. The fact that I can make him talk, and frequently do by opening the catch on the underside of his mouth, might, admittedly be construed as being a little quirky, and that time I wore him round my neck to the co-op didn't seem to go down too well at all, but I wish you could see him, really I do, he's lovely and soft and he does a great line at parties.

I was once the proud owner of a rather splendid stuffed Lapwing. I first fell in love with him in a junk shop in Canterbury, and as I felt like he deserved a chance (although in what exactly I'm not sure), I gave the stallholder £10 and he was mine. I felt he was well worth the money, because although he had obviously met his match violently in some way, judging from his manky, deformed side, his good side more than compensated for this. (I suppose there is only so much you can do with taxidermy anyway). Owing to his obviously adventuresome life and even more audacious death, I decided to call him William the Conqueror. Do you know, I loved that bird. I displayed him proudly (good side out) wherever I happened to be living. He even accompanied me to workshops on several occasions, as a muse for the groups to draw, until I got so fed up hearing them all whining on about him, "urgh it smells" and "take that thing away, I'm not drawing that", that his modelling career was cut short and I put him back on my shelf at home where he remained, until I noticed one day that all his little feathers were falling out. I wept as I carried him out to the wheelie bin in his black bin liner burial shroud.

I would just like to point out that actually, taxidermy is 'in' at the moment.

I did once have a fungus the bogeyman hot-water bottle that I could make look like it was being sick, but these were isolated incidences so it would be unfair for you to allow them to colour your judgement of me.

*   *   *

Since I've lived in Wales, the place has got under my skin. The Welsh have a name for it 'Hiraeth' which means a sort of longing, like a homesickness for the land when you are away from it. Any ancient places or landscapes seem to have a presence that can pull you in; I think that's why I loved living in Canterbury so much, all those vibes from the past, alright, many involving ducking stools and murderers, but nevertheless part of our rich heritage.

More than probably it is the land here in Gwynedd

which finally claimed me as its own and has helped me to at last feel that this is home. I don't know whether being an artist makes me more susceptible to this kind of thing, but I do know that when I am painting, a part of me seems to be functioning on a subconscious level, and not always after a few glasses of wine. I would say that the act of painting, apart from the obvious practical skills, involves the use of part intellect and part instinct. When I am working I'm using my head and my heart and my hand is merely the tool I need in order to execute the painting.

Whilst addressing a group of people recently, several of them said that my work had a 'Welshness' about it and that they could see the influence of my surroundings in it. I was a bit surprised because I hadn't realised quite how much the place had crept up on me over the years of living here.

I was asked a few years ago, to take part in a themed exhibition, 'Welsh Artists Abroad' and although I might not be 'officially Welsh' I felt that I had served enough time here to be awarded the title of 'honorary Welsh tart', as my brother-in-law likes to put it. Anyway, not wanting to miss out, I agreed to participate. There was just one little problem ……..

If you don't include my moving from England to Wales, I had not set foot on foreign soil for approximately thirty years, in fact not since the time when I'd had a 'proper job'. Yet still, I was determined.

Oh, I could just imagine it all, with the participating artists outdoing each other with their exotic landscapes, depicting scenes from recent …… I find it hard to get the word out ……. holidays. "Yes, I did this one while I was painting my toenails, sipping my G&T and steering the gondola in the Himalayas" and here's a little sketch that I did on the bloody moon", but hey, I'm not bitter.

With a flash of inspiration I realized that I could get around this problem by, well, lying, and that I could hold the world, if not in the palm of my hand, then certainly at the end of a brush, in my fingertips. I would go to the airport. I would hold my head up amongst all those smug well travelled bastards that I hadn't had the wherewithal to compete with. There is nothing more tedious than being in the company of people that spend an entire evening blathering on about whether Egypt has the edge over Malaya, or their experience in Timbuktu, when you can't even run to a weekend in Clamping. Never heard of it? There you are, I rest my case.

Obviously, I would need to employ a considerable amount of artistic licence here. I planned my trip with the zeal of a researcher for Lonely Planet. Blimey, I realised, I could go anywhere I wanted ……. in the world.

After wrestling with Mumbai and the West Indies, I decided that some of the Mediterranean resorts might be a bit more believable and would be easier to find reference for, then I could just copy the scenes from a library book without too much effort, (I am coming back as a sloth in my next life). The really great thing about this sort of travelling is that you don't have to go through all that palaver at the airport, you don't get jet-lag, and you don't have to agonize over what to pack; plus you are unlikely to contract Beri-Beri disease whilst sitting watching Eastenders in your living room.

I didn't really like the idea of having to rely on someone else's reference in the form of books and magazines etc., it was reminding me of the 'Labradors in the basket' time all those years ago, but what choice did I have.

I quickly discovered that painting landscapes that I had never seen, let alone spent time in, was actually not much fun. My efforts were looking as stilted as the photographs I was working from, and it soon became apparent that I was not going to impress anyone.

The deciding factor in abandoning this approach came with the realization (why hadn't I thought of this earlier?) that not only would I finish up with some nasty dull paintings, but that I would not be able to turn up at the preview and swan around like I normally do, as I would be terrified that sooner or later someone would quiz me about my amazing travels and realise that my body of work was in fact a pack of lies, and that I was a fraud, a saddo that had had to resort to such underhand measures, just so that I could be in with the 'golden globetrotters'. No, this would not do, just one little slip-up would expose me for the charlatan that I undoubtedly am.

Chameleon-like, I quickly changed tack and settled on another way to infiltrate the inner circle. I decided that if I was going to cheat, I might as well do it for all to see, and do it with panache and humour. Yes, I would make a virtue of my lack of worldliness, so I set about planning a small series of paintings depicting me on a tongue-in-cheek gastronomical tour, encompassing a few European destinations.

I had lots of fun on my travels: I painted myself behind an enormous plate of spaghetti, with hands that had morphed into pigs trotters in Italy. Whilst 'off-piste' in Austria I found myself stuffing a large cream confection into my face, and in Rome I was found draped around a naked stone Adonis with several bottles of plonk around my feet. My journey ended with me having put on several stone in weight by this time, looking fat, blotchy and moony-eyed in Spain, being fed ice-cream off a spoon by a greasy wop with blue-black hair, a whiter than white smile and a gold medallion.

I tell you the paintings went down a storm, I had depicted myself swollen with gluttony and now I was swollen with pride.

Whenever I feel complacent, or smug, or think that I've got away with something, there will always be some glitch that will spoil things and my little ruse will come back to bite me on the bum. Why doesn't this happen to other people, why is it always me that is doomed to a life of staying on the straight and narrow, for fear of being caught out. I have persistently tried to err from the path of righteousness and get away with it, but I am always hauled back.

Just as I was thinking I'd pulled it off and deflected the interest away from the fact that I had been nowhere, and was undoubtedly going nowhere, my little ruse backfired. I'd been quietly chuckling to myself about the great compliments I was receiving about the paintings and had even managed to sell a few, when the cold cold dawn of cruel realization began to infiltrate my sad little mind and inflated ego. When I tell you that in reality I am size 10 -12 (ok occasionally a 14) dress size, you will start to realize how shocking and upsetting it was to receive such compliments as, "Oh, we could see it was you straight away", and "how did you manage to get such a good likeness of yourself", and "your not THAT fat". It is important that you remember here that I had depicted myself growing increasingly grotesque as the tour progressed, finishing with me looking like an overfed, debauched porker.

To sum up the experience, I realized sadly, that now I was no longer just on the outside without a ticket, looking into the bus of global trotters, having still not actually been anywhere, but that I was also, a fat, bloated, old soak, peering longingly through the bus window as it was moving off to more exotic pastures once again.

The only small ray of hope that I can hang onto is that I'm thinking that of course I don't really look like I'd portrayed myself in the pictures, (do I?) but I do love food, so maybe I'd somehow managed to portray the inner pig in me that was obviously trying to get out, and this had come across as a likeness in the paintings. What do you think? Please allow me to believe in myself again, and not feel that I do actually look like a mochyn.

* * *

If you've been paying attention and haven't glazed over by now and your not a lazy reader like me, whereby I have a tendency to skim over words that I don't understand and move onto the next bit, or that indeed you are not Welsh, you may well be wondering what the word at the end of the last paragraph means. Mochyn. That's 'pig' to you. Yes, mochyn is the Welsh word for pig, and it is at this point that I would like to digress for a few moments, and address the little issue of language that can arise when living in a foreign place.

Now I am definitely not of the same mind as a past neighbour of mine who once said "I don't know why the bloody Welsh can't just pull themselves together and speak properly, (presumably this meant speaking

English with a Brummie accent like him). I imagine if he had hailed from Italy he would have had the Welsh all speaking Italian. He then embarked on a diatribe of the shortfalls of Welsh people speaking their own language in their own country ..... well yes, what a cheek, until he noticed my expression and suddenly stopped mid sentence and promptly changed tack.

I admit, the Welsh language can be a problem when ordering stuff over the phone. I once lived in a place where my address was so difficult to get across that I had to make the conversation into a sort of word game and use the same kind of slow, deliberate voice that is used when speaking to idiots, in order to get the person at the other end to understand .... H for Harry, E for end, N for normal, L for let's just forget it shall we, because by the time you get to the end you've forgotten what you wanted to order anyway.

Anyway, the fact is I had made my home in Wales, and I am of a mind that if you choose to live in a place, it is good to make at least a bit of an effort in getting to grips with the lingo; also, the Welsh language is a rich and ancient part of the culture here, so it is important to keep it alive. Wales is a bi-lingual country so I don't feel that it is essential for everyone living here to zealously rush out and learn Welsh, but I do feel that it is worth making the effort to at least be able to pronounce the name of the village that you live in. I know quite a few incomers that can't, some of which have been here for forty years.

Yes, I can pronounce the name of my village, and yes, I have acquired a good vocabulary, and yes, my pronunciation isn't bad. Yet still I can't string more than the shortest sentences together. It's hard! I did attend a Welsh course a few years ago for a short time, but in the end there were only two of us turning up. I actually felt very sorry for the teacher, because the fact is, her only surviving students were probably about the worst out of the original group. As we spent much of the lessons giggling nervously, when we got it wrong yet again, I did wonder if we were in fact part of the reason for the others departure.

Our teacher was young, vibrant and full of fun, but her day job was to teach infant school children who were like annoying little sponges when it came to soaking up information at lightening speed. Most of us in the evening class really could have done with going at the sort of pace you would use for severely damaged stroke victims, but we tried our best to soldier on.

She would put us into small groups and get us to form sentences that told a little story; the showy-off know-it-all's would come up with nice neat little phrases like :

'Helo Dafydd, onid yw hyn yn rhan hyfryd o'r byd, ydych chi wedi byw yma o hyd? A fyddwch yn gyrru i'r farchnad heddiw i brynu rhai nwyddau gyda Megan y ci defaid?'

('Hello David, what a lovely part of the world this is,

131

have you lived here long? Will you be driving to the market today to buy some groceries with Megan the sheepdog?')

Naturally, I would always finish up with the duffers in the naughty group, where we would attempt to hide our inadequacies by resorting to pathetic childish humour :

'Daf, fyddwn I hoffi weld ti eto, ond yn gyntaf oll, hoffwn I wybod os oes gen ti swydd? Wyt ti'n berchen ar dy cartref dy hun? – ac a oes gen ti pidyn mawr?')

('Dave, I would quite like to see you again, but first of all I would like to know if you have a job? – do you own your own home? – and have you got a big willy?')

I always meant to practice during the week, I really did, but I was easily put off when I would proudly recite my latest conquests to any poor sod that kept still for long enough, only to be met with a blank stare of incomprehension. My boss in college threatened, no sorry, I mean offered, to send me on one of those intense short courses, where you live, eat and breath Welsh for a few days and an undercover spy follows you around to make sure you are conversing in Welsh at all times. I did seriously toy with the idea until I learnt from a colleague that the learners were being forced to do 'country dancing' as part of a team building exercise. No, I would have to conquer this on my own.

I began to realise that my enthusiasm to practice was

not shared by everyone, when at the end of yet another lunchtime session in the staff room, of me making whichever unlucky colleagues that happened to be present test me, one chap said despairingly "for God's sake Wendy give it a rest". Sniff.

Living on my own, I would take any opportunity to practice when in company, but the futility of this started to become apparent when I found that I could ask anyone a question, but would be totally floored if they said anything back. I realized I was flogging a dead horse one day, when I asked a friend if he wanted 'sex' in his drink instead of 'ice', and I sadly came to the conclusion that I would more than probably never experience the satisfaction of conversing in Welsh.

*   *   *

Now, where was I? After roaming around the peripheries of the Welsh language, back to the expectations that are placed on me as an artist.

I have found during my time as a painter that there are some very common misconceptions that are associated with the artist's life.

When people that I have not met before ask what I do for a living, (as if the knitted skirt wasn't a big enough clue), when I tell them I'm a painter, they get a sort of glazed, hazy look come over them, smile knowingly, and say "oh, how lovely, aren't you lucky". My immediate reaction to this guff is to want to punch them in the face. Yet I have to say that in some ways they are right. On the odd occasions when the work is going well and the creative juices are flowing, it can feel like the best job in the world, plus I am extremely lucky to have found the thing that I feel pretty sure I am meant to be doing. I have the freedom to work from home, and part of my work involves me going out and about, roaming around taking photographs and sketching, which in theory should be enjoyable. Unfortunately I am a 'puritan' at heart so I usually spend at least half of this stage feeling guilty that I am not 'suffering' enough.

Right, that's enough of the me being ever so lucky bit. There is a big BUT on the way. What people often don't realize is that doing anything creative for a living is very different from doing something creative as a hobby, and it comes with certain trials and tribulations. Creating something from scratch for anyone, can be hard and often agonizing and is certainly not something which flows miraculously from the fingertips, no matter how much natural ability the artist may have been born with.

There is nothing more terrifying than being faced with a 'blank' anything, whether it be a screen, a piece of paper, a canvas or a stage. I imagine part of the terror one feels is to do with the not knowing if the piece you have been working on for days, and in my case throwing shed loads of paint at, will turn out ok or not. I see each painting that I do as a production, a subjective dramatization of the familiar things around me. I tell you, it's a monumental task to attempt to re-create the world in the way I want to see it, so you will understand how nerve-wracking it can be.

If I was doing some sort of craft, I would need skill and dexterity, but the chances are I'd be following a recipe or have a pattern or plan to guide me, but anything that is a one-off original means that 'you're on your own kid', so the responsibility is all yours – there is no-one else to blame when it all goes wrong.

It's amazing the lengths one can go to in order to avoid in my case, the terror of crossing the threshold of my studio; all those incredibly tedious little jobs that you never quite get round to doing, like sorting out your sock drawer or visiting someone you can't stand, suddenly become attractively imperative. I have even been known to DUST rather than face the music.

I know that working from home sounds idyllic, and in some ways it is great; you can convince yourself that you really deserve to have a lie-in and take an hour and a half for lunch …. again. But, if like me, you have the self-discipline of a peanut, it can prove to be a bit of a problem. Other people too, can't seem to get it into their heads that even though you may not have actually left the house, you are in fact, at least pretending to work. I suppose part of the problem is that 'doing art' can be a hobby and it can be quite hard for civilians to understand that it can also be a job.

I used to live in a bungalow where my studio was part of an extension on the back, with large picture windows. An artist friend of mine would on occasions come round and do 'spot checks' by creeping round the back and peering in through the studio window to see if I was working. I lived in terror of turning round and finding her looming outside (she is tall).

*   *   *

It seems to be quite common for artists to be perceived as having a bit of a chequered image when seen through the eyes of some civilians.

Everyone loves the romantic idea of the scruffy artist, starving in a garret, well, everyone except the artist that is. As a breed we are often expected to be a bit odd, on the edge, outside the peripheries of decent society, and people can be bitterly disappointed if they suspect us of 'being normal', heaven forbid.

I have to admit, that during my years of working as a painter, I have frequently played to the crowd and 'milked' this notion of being seen as an oddball. The fact is, we as artists can get away with, if not murder, quite a lot of stuff that civilians can't.

If I have a talk looming up, I can often be found wandering around the hills above where I live and 'practicing' (out loud). Locals are used to me by now and just say "oh it's alright, its only Wendy, that artist". Admittedly, if I am caught out by visitors to the area, they can look a bit alarmed and no doubt put me down as the local nutter. It used to be quite handy when I had a dog because I could pretend to be talking to her whenever I was caught out, although anyone hearing a snippet of my soliloquy might have thought it odd that a sheepdog would be interested in 3-point perspective.

I was merrily stomping along one day, on one of my walks, muttering with my head down, as I practiced for a forthcoming talk, when I looked up to see a massive bull, just inches (oh alright a few feet) from me, staring through mean little piggy eyes. I believe that I came very close to having a heart attack as I flung myself down the hill on jelly legs, crying and swearing like a demented creature. When I realized that I couldn't hear the beast thundering behind me, I stopped and looked back up the hill to see the demon standing staring at me in exactly the same position like a big teddy-bear, looking bemused.

I am not adverse to 'hamming it up' when it comes to the clichéd, rather scatterbrained, disorganized image that some people associate with the artist …. when it suits me. If I don't feel like tidying-up, (which is all the time really), I know I can get away with it. Civilians will look adoringly at my squalor and say "oh, you artists" ...... it's great!

In reality, I might not love housework, but I am one of the most organized people I know. My work space is not that messy and on occasions I have resorted to 'distressing it' a little prior to someone visiting in order not to disappoint the public in their expectations of my arty image. There is nothing more dispiriting than a tidy art studio.

I realize that in writing this I am exposing myself as a bit of a fraud, and I am really sorry if I am shattering anyone's illusions, but I have to confess that I like nice things; I love clothes and I like wearing make-up and perfume. Alright, the make-up is no longer Clarins, and most of my clothes are from charity shops (you may want to pause to get a tissue here), but it's surprising what you can do with some Dylon and a bit of flair.

Lavinia (her of the dummies) and I have become slaves to the bottle, that's fake suntan, as well as Vodka. I know this doesn't really go with the arty image and might in fact be more appropriate if we were married to successful footballers, but there we are, I am being honest here. Since holidays in Barbados are no longer on the agenda, it's Costa del Superdrug for the tan these days. For several summers we have floated, we thought rather glamorously, around the village, in our little shorts with our sketchbooks tucked underneath our arms, posing as weather browned artists, until her son rather cruelly said one day, that we looked like a couple of smoked kippers.

The fact is, despite the orange legs, I am totally committed to my work, but when it comes to my image I draw the line at crocheted skirts and rainbow hair. While I'm on a roll in exposing the real me and shattering your idea of me as a painter, I have a shocking confession to make. Now, I am not proud of this, but despite the fact that I know I am expected to be so intense, sensitive and 'other worldly' for such earthly delights, if I was faced with a choice between a cultural trip to a museum or art gallery or a trip to John Lewis, I'm afraid I would 'forever knowingly sell my soul'. On days when there is a shopping trip in the offing I rise up with a spring in my step.

Yet despite this, it seems that the inner artist will out in the end, no matter how hard I may try to pretend to be normal. One of the nicest things anyone ever said to me was that I looked like my work. I took this in the spirit of which I am fairly sure it was intended to be taken, as a compliment, and not that they saw me as a sloppy, dribbling mess.

As I said before, I am just as guilty of putting people into boxes as the next person. A friend of mine was once asked to do a workshop for a group of people staying at an artistic spiritual retreat, whatever in the world that meant. We discussed the possibilities that this conjured up and expecting organic turps and knitted aprons, we decked her out in socks and sandals and a voluminous skirt borrowed from her mother's wardrobe, adding a finishing touch by tying a scarf round her head (well she likes to fit in). My parting words were "mind they don't brainwash you". The poor girl was mortified when upon meeting the group for the first time she was confronted by a load of bright, trendy designers wearing what looked suspiciously like Louis Vuitton overalls.

Although I myself may have strayed at times from the look that is expected of me, any artists out there that do wish to be 'purists' in terms of flying the flag of the arty-farty image will find my little compendium of 'artist tips' invaluable. Yes, if you want to 'look the part' you won't go far wrong if you follow these general rules of dress conduct and you will be assured of forever living up to 'normal peoples' expectations:

It's simple really, the no-no's or things to avoid if you don't want to end up looking like a civilian are as follows :

- Anything which looks reasonable or average (yuck).

- Avoid any item of clothing which looks 'normal' (unless you team it with something outrageous like a stuffed ferret).

- Absolutely never touch beige, and never ever harmonize colours together.

- Nothing flashy or smacking of 'designer'; this is extended to vehicles; in fact if you can get hold of an old van and paint flowers and 'save our planet' messages on it all the better). The fact that the emissions from this rust bucket are powerful enough to propel a turbo powered space rocket is neither here nor there, it's the look that counts.

- Obviously avoid anything which looks sensible or fashionable and it goes without saying that 'tasteful' is a dirty word.

You are more than probably feeling a bit lost and disillusioned by now, but cheer-up because I've taken the trouble to come up with some very useful 'yes's' for you to choose from. Here they are:

Basically, any items of clothing that you put together are acceptable if they have:

- Clashing colours.

- Rips, holes or uneven hemlines.

- Creases; these have to be genuine and not those designer creases that you get in some 'tasteful' garments.

- Anything misshapen, (preferably knitted).

- Anything with bits of cotton or wool hanging from it or better still has mirrors on.

- A slightly grubby look can be good, (remember you don't want to wash away your natural oils) and if you must wash, make sure you only use soap that smells like it has been made from organic sewage; either that or doesn't smell of anything at all.

Don't whatever you do, fall into the trap, like several artists I have known, of dressing snappily and even with panache, or, dare I say it …. Smartly; not if you don't want to let the side down and ruin other peoples' expectations of the arty image.

I have admitted that I myself, may have strayed on occasions from the evangelical path of 'le Poseur', but don't fret, you've only to visit me at home and see my paint-smeared door handles and stuffed crow hanging from the hall light fitting, to be reassured that I am indeed an artist.

If you are still struggling, although I see so reason why you would be after that lot, remember that if you do find yourself in danger of looking 'normal', adding a plastic parrot or a flamboyant flower to the shoulder of your outfit can disguise even the most pedestrian of outfits.

I hope you appreciate the fact that I'm going the extra mile for you here in giving away many of the gems that my years of experience have provided me with.

Oh what the hell, I'm feeling generous, so here are a few more words of wisdom:

It's not enough to simply look the part, if you are to be taken seriously as an 'artist' you need to start behaving like one too:

For instance turning up late (for anything), (funerals included, well you won't be offending the dead person will you), is an absolute must. If you can manage outrageously late, all the better. I have really had to work on myself for this one. I am unfortunately the sort of person that tends to arrive annoyingly on time and on occasions unforgivably early, then I am the last to leave, in fact I am often thrown out. I really do try to be late, but it's hard.

As far as behaviour goes generally, basically any outrageous / bad / gross / debauched / promiscuous conduct is good news; or if you prefer you can go for the holier-than-thou stance, where you get rid of your telly, spurn all Christmas and birthday presents as being too consumerist, read all the self-help books you can lay your hands on and only ever put pure, organic substances down your smug little throat. Personally I've always favoured the former approach.

There isn't a lot I can say about the sort of food you need to be seen to be eating, except that it should be wholesome and tasteless, oh, and it should look ghastly. Basically any mass of organic (with a capital O) matter, that is grey and cooked in a large dubious looking pot that may have come from an archaeological dig, on top of the stove for several hours, and served with a haunch of dense wholemeal bread that is so dry you will need hydrotherapy if you are ever to swallow again, is good. Wash this down with organic beetroot juice or ragwort and bluebottle tea served in a hand-made mug that looks like it has been fashioned out of hardened porridge, and your image is complete …… or almost; if you can enlist the help of a breastfeeding mother to join you and your chums around the scrubbed pine table, that would be great. The older the infant the better, fourteen is pushing it, but a six year old is ideal.

Just one more tiny thing. If you can't get to live in a dilapidated mansion that you share with a load of strangers, you can transform an otherwise boring semi by draping Indian prayer flags around the greenhouse.

Seriously though, fellow sufferers, if you are feeling a bit overwhelmed by all the arty criteria which you will be expected to adhere to if you are to be taken seriously as a 'proper artist, the one thing that will speed you on your way to taking your place at the top of the 'I'm a fabulous artist scale', is to make sure your latest project contains reference to some kind of detritus in the title. 'Waste' or 'Decay' are key suggestions; this can be particularly appropriate if the final product finishes up looking like a pile of shit.

If all else fails you can always draw comfort from having a 'group hug' with your artist playmates.

Of course, it would have been so much easier in the

past, to maintain the bohemian lifestyle. For a start, I would have had much easier access to Absinthe. You can't find it for love nor money these days, despite me asking Morrisons if they could order some in for me; they just look at me blankly and try palming me off with gin or vodka, but it just won't do.

Being poor, does at least allow me to stay true to some of the criteria that goes hand in hand with being a real bohemian; and I wish I could say that I didn't give a monkey's about what anyone thought of me, which is another prerequisite, but alas that wouldn't be strictly true.

I don't mind telling you, it's not easy these days to be a purist when it comes to the arty image. It's so much harder to shock now, than it was in the times when there were stricter rules of conduct; with even civilians adopting weird lifestyle choices and trying to nudge artists out of the way when it comes to the shockability factor. One of the local undertakers, (I say one, because death is quite big here), has been spotted on several occasions, sporting a pink velour tracksuit whilst visiting bereaved relatives. This is the same chap, whose mobile phone once went off in the middle of a funeral that I was attending, to the tune of 'Mission Impossible'; but to give him credit, he did look mortified.

The thing though that has really thrown a spanner in the works, is the National Health Service. It is virtually impossible these days to die tragically young and to suffer with a consumptive cough, whilst ruining countless frilly white hankies with blood spots. It's just not the same with Kleenex extra strong. Remedies for this, remedies for that. You try having an attack of the vapours today, and all you get is "pull yourself together".

Artists are constantly having to keep one step ahead of the game, by inventing new ways to be tragic and to be seen as being odd, while civilians are trying to jump on our band wagon. Stick to your bloody grey suits can't you.

One gallery owner I know, referred fondly back to the good old days, when artists lived up to their image of being outrageous, eccentric weirdo's; "They're all so boring and normal these days" she lamented, after attending an arty soiree, "it was more like a confederation of accountants". I have to say, I agree; hard work though it is sometimes, I do feel it is our duty to keep our reputation going before it is too late and we all slip into 'tastefulness' erughhh.

*   *   *

We artists can be notoriously bad at 'selling ourselves', we are of course much too 'other-worldly' and sensitive for such crude matters ...... when it suits us. I do think that very generally speaking there is a grain of truth in this; on the whole, many of us aren't that good at promoting ourselves. However, it has to be said that there are exceptions to this notion, in reality I know of several such angelic souls that would easily eclipse a rampaging herd of rhinos when it comes to trampling over anything and anyone that dares to get in the way of them reaching whatever goal they are aiming after, but I would say they are fairly unusual.

Now, I am definitely not ruthless, and although I would like to make it to the first division, I would prefer to take a few friends with me. I am however, strong and determined, blimey, let's face it I must be to have survived as an artist for as long as I have, although I suppose this could be attributed more to bloody-mindedness. Yet despite this, I find that when I need to make contact with certain galleries, I suddenly find myself turning into a snivelling, sycophantic wreck. If I wasn't holding the phone in one hand, I'm sure there would be a lot of wringing and rubbing of hands, Uriah Heap style, going on during conversations where I find myself obsequiously thanking the person on the other end of the phone, for not offering me a solo show and for hanging my work directly under the sign for the toilets, (still I suppose it could be worse). I have tried the usual things, like imagining the person on the other end of the phone naked etc. but if I know that they happen to be an attractive bloke, this just makes it worse.

It's odd really, because I am not consistent in this self-deprecating attitude to myself; maybe it's the old show-off trying to get out again.

I know it's not the done thing, and you may be shocked to hear this, but I LIKE PREVIEWS. There, it's out. It is of course fashionable to say "oh no, I never go to previews, I'm only interested in 'doing' the work", and most self-respecting artists will tell you that they only attend them out of a sense of obligation or under duress. Not me, I love em. Hell, what's not to like? You turn up in a nice frock (well maybe not if you are a man, but do feel free if you would like to), then you get your free glass of wine (two if you pretend to be getting one for a friend as well), and swan around for a couple of hours while people lie about how much they 'luuurrve' your work darrrling. They'll make a big show of saying "we think your work is by far the best in the exhibition" before scurrying off to buy someone else's, but just for those few deluded moments while they're sucking up, you allow yourself to enjoy all the attention.

No, previews are the nice easy part, it's doing the work that's the pain in the arse. I sometimes think that certain contemporary artists have the right idea by following in Michelangelo's footsteps, and getting minions to do the hard work for them. Anyway, how hard can it be to unscrew the lid on a jar of pickling vinegar?

HOW LONG DID IT TAKE?

Wendy Murphy

So, we've established that artists can get away with a lot more stuff than civilians would be able to. If I'm honest I could almost feel a bit sorry for you lot out there, and even grateful at times, for putting up with having to live alongside us weirdos.

How many other sectors of society could expect such a modest reaction, of merely benign bewilderment, or at the very worst irritated intolerance, in response to having presented to the world, scenes of violence, debauched cherubs or naked women being served drinks from scantily clad slaves, under the guise of 'Art'.

It is to civilians' credit, that most of you seem to be, if not a little reluctantly, just resigned, in accepting the 'Hoover in the Perspex case', the 'window mounted roadkill', and the 'burnt dismembered teddies', as the annoying but harmless offerings of those members of society that are strange, rather than suggesting that it must be the work of perverts and psychopaths, which let's face would be the case in any other area of life.

I would like to say thank-you, for not insisting that we be locked up in high security institutions.

It's not like I am not aware, or even sympathetic, to the position you are in. Let's face it, you're damned if you do and you're damned if you don't. When you tell us 'arty' lot that you really love our work, we think you are being patronising and are just saying it to flatter us; but if you dare to criticise our efforts, we call you bastards and accuse you of being visually illiterate. Probably best just to keep mum, although even this might be read as callous indifference. Just remember, you are dealing with the artistic temperament here, so tread carefully.

Yet no matter how much I am aware of the civilian predicament, I have to say that they don't always make it easy on themselves. For a start they can be incredibly contrary creatures. If they discover a painting in their attic they want it to be worth millions, but, if they see a painting on a gallery wall, they want to get it for a song. Similarly, they will tell you how much they like to support the arts, and how much they love your work, but when it comes to coughing-up they will try to brow-beat you into letting them have a painting for such a little amount of money, that your share won't even cover your petrol in getting to the gallery. Oh and by the way, this is the same person that has just spent the last hour telling you about their holiday home in the Sechelles, their rental apartments in France and London, and the various holidays they have just booked, before you make your way back home to your rented bed-sit.

Someone that may know very little about art, or painting, as a subject, will suddenly become an expert when it comes to proffering a critique on a piece of artwork.

Don't get me wrong, I know that art appreciation is

subjective, and of course everyone is entitled to their tastes and opinions. It is the aggressive certainty of their knowledge regarding the quality of a painting, which I find hard to accept.

I am not really into poetry. I am not proud of this fact, but as to date it hasn't particularly grabbed me, so I accept that my knowledge of this genre is limited to say the least, and the type of verse that I'm likely to appreciate is, unfortunately, of the 'There was a young man from Bodmin' variety. Therefore I wouldn't dream of going up to Carol Anne Duffy and saying "excuse me love, but that's just rubbish", because I can't appreciate or relate to something she has written. I hold my hands up, I can see that the fault is with me, rather than her, but it's surprising how many uninformed civilians will state in no uncertain terms that an artist's work is a load of rubbish.

Now, this is the important thing, you are allowed to say that in your opinion you think it's a load of tosh, but not that it is a load of tosh …….. there's a huge difference. Of course there is a lot of work out there that is a load of tosh, but that's beside the point.

This same person will then go on to tell you what is good. I have learnt to be on the alert for the hand, sliding John Wayne style, slyly into a side pocket in order to fish out a phone containing numerous (and I mean numerous) images of their own ghastly paintings, which you are expected to coo over.

When I was still a student and before the days when I had become 'soft' and opted for working from the comfort of my studio, I was often to be found perched outside on my fishing stool, vigilantly drawing and painting. The response to this by onlookers was varied. In one camp there were the awe-struck lot that gazed at you in wonder and thought you were marvellous just because you had a pencil stuck behind your ear. These were great, because it didn't matter if what you had produced was crap, this lot wouldn't have known the difference anyway and the sheer fact of you being there and doing it gave you credibility in their eyes. These were the ego-strokers that almost had you believing yourself that what you had produced was good.

Then there were the OTHERS (this is another instance where shakey letters and dripping blood might be appropriate). This group tended to comprise most of the population that were in the same vicinity as yourself on that particular day. They were the one's that would stand so close to you that on many occasions you would feel them leaning against your back and their hot fiery breath on the back of your neck. After standing there silently for twenty minutes or so, they would then begin the predictable build-up of how they themselves couldn't draw a straight line, (well why the dickens should they be able to, I can't add up but I don't keep wittering on about it). This little soliloquy would invariably end with them telling you about their 3-yr old nephew/grandchild/godson who was absolutely brilliant at art but how his sister didn't have an artistic bone in her body but whose parents had been told by the school's head-teacher that Stephanie was actually too clever for her class and should be moved up a year which the family had always suspected would be the case and did I think that artistic genius could skip a few generations or not and might not it be just possible that granddad Bert who had lost his leg in France might be responsible for passing on the artistic gene or did I think it was from aunty Nora whose father wouldn't let her go to art school because of the family sweet shop…..

By this time of course I would have lost the plot regarding my drawing, although it has to be said, I had gained inside knowledge of members of a family that I had never met, so that's good isn't it.

I would often be repaid for my rapt attention by my new friend looking scornfully over my shoulder at my abandoned efforts before sniffing and shuffling off, muttering 'even our Stephanie could have done better than that'.

I learnt to develop 'a look' which would send them scurrying off in terror. Wearing headphones was also a good idea, even if you weren't actually listening to anything, as you could pretend to be deaf when necessary.

Those were the days when I would take to the road on my rather expensive pushbike that I had purchased from Harrods during the time when I'd had a proper job. I would load up my panniers with every single bit of art equipment that I owned, and spend the day roaming around the countryside, searching for the perfect spot to paint, which was always just over the brow of the next hill, and feeling guilty that a) I hadn't yet found it, b) I wasn't actually working, and c) the only effort I had put in during my 'working trip' was when I'd stopped to eat my sandwiches for half an hour at lunchtime.

I would invariably finish up returning to my lodgings at the end of the day with a pathetic little sketch that I'd done 5 minutes before nightfall, where my housemates would be waiting with a large glass of wine and a disproportionate amount of praise for my efforts.

Still, the exercise was good I suppose, and I developed calf muscles that had been laying dormant (a legacy from my father) and which have remained with me to the present day. Thanks Dad. It is not easy going through life with Queen Anne table legs. Pity really, I hadn't been better at sports, I might have made the English women's football team.

*   *   *

Don't get me wrong, I am not really a 'civilian hater', remember I was one once. I know that many of the ridiculous comments they come out with are born not out of unkindness, but stem from an unawareness of what living the life of an artist actually entails.

Yet despite this, I have been surprised and even shocked on occasions, at the thoughtlessness that I have experienced at the hands of quite a large proportion of the non-artist population, but maybe I just haven't been mixing in the right circles.

It is quite common for civilians to imagine that as an artist, you must be leading the life of Riley and don't know the meaning of the word 'work'. I can tell you that when you've been working your butt off for nearly thirty years, much of that time without being paid, this attitude can stick in your craw.

A typical conversation between an artist and a civilian may run something like this :

After the initial introductions have been made;

A. "so what do you do"?

Civ. "I work in I.T. In fact I've just got to the top of my tree with the company I've been with for the last five years, so I'm setting up my own consultancy where I'll be making an absolute mint from just advising people where to stick their laptops, and of course they'll be lots of opportunity to ....

There is usually a considerable amount of time spent at this point in the monologue, sorry, I mean conversation, with me standing listening and making a polite response every now and then, (although this is not strictly necessary, because this type doesn't need feedback once he's off on one). While the civ. has had more than their fair share of the craic, you have reached that stage where you have glazed over to such an extent that you are close to transcending into the realms of 'Nirvana'. Then just before you slip into unconscious bliss, you will be pulled cruelly back to earth, when you realize that civ has popped the ball over the net and is letting you have a go. He has asked a question...... yeeeees!

You are not really on your best form by this time, because you have forgotten what your own name is, but damnit, you're blowed if you're going to pass up this opportunity to speak. The conversation continues :

Civ. "What about you, what do you do for a living?"

"Oh, I'm a painter actually" (forget it love if you are expecting any kind of   admiration, or even interest for that matter.)

Civ. "Oh really? How much do you charge?" - "The reason I ask is that Merrily and I were thinking of having the lounge re-painted."

A. "No no, I mean I'm a painter, as in artist."

Civ."Oh right, (yawn). So tell me, what do you do?"

A. "Well, I've just said, I'm a painter."

Civ. "Yes, but what job do you do?"

"I'm a professional painter, that is my job?"

"Right ……. and do you work as well?"

Here are a few more of my favourite civvy quotes :

"Oh well, it's lucky you don't need as much money if you are an artist do you".

"Oh well, you don't need as much money if you live in the country do you".

"Have you ever worked"?

"Ever had a 'proper job"?

"Do you work as well"?

"Ha ha ha ho heeeee ha ha ooh sorry, but artists are meant to be hard-up aren't they."

"Still dabbling"?

"Cor, you lot have a life of Riley don't ya".

"You must show me your 'bits' sometime". (Do you think they meant my paintings)?

"Have you thought of displaying your work in that new junk shop that's just opened in Tywyn, he's looking for some pictures to fill up the walls".

"Have you thought of showing your work on the internet" (do you honestly think I wouldn't have thought of every bloody thing).

"What about a car boot sale"? (What about a car boot sale?)

This one after having just spent five years doing hard labour at art college: "what you gonna do with that then?"

But I've saved the most common, and by far my favourite, until last :

"Look on the bright side luvvie, you'll be rich and famous after your dead". (This one is nearly always accompanied by raucous laughter and on one occasion, slapping me on the back.)

Yea, what a hoot. How many other professions do you know of where you are encouraged to look forward to your death.

*   *   *

An elderly relative of Mihangel's, visiting us one day at the medieval death trap, expressed a wish to see my studio. After some considerable time and effort, negotiating the steep, winding staircase, we managed to push and pull her up the last few treads, before the three of us staggered like a big breathless, wobbling jelly into my lonely eyrie where we wedged her into a chair.

She spent the next half hour contemplating a couple of quite nice flower paintings that I just happened to have propped up against the wall and I was convinced a sale was 'in the bag', particularly as I'd plied her with tea, cakes and sherry and was well aware that she wasn't short of a bob or two. On reflection, I think she was probably just playing for time and getting her equilibrium back before having to face the stairs again, because she eventually looked up, beamed at me, and said "I like the frames".

I decided at the time, to spare aunty Minnie from the firing squad, come the Revolution, because, God love her, this was a woman whose eyesight had become so bad whilst she was awaiting a cataract operation, that she bought an eight-year old boy a mug for his birthday with 'You're a Star' written on one side, and 'World's Best Dad' on the other.

This had followed an earlier incident where she had

161

spent over forty minutes enticing 'Fluffy' in for the night, before realising she had been talking to a large stone at the end of the path.

*   *   *

Negative comments can be more of a danger to beginners just starting out and needing all the encouragement they can get, than they are to hardy old pro's like myself. I was giving a talk fairly recently to an art group, about my experience as an artist. I was just telling them that I'd had to toughen up, and what I thought I'd said, was that during my time as an artist I'd had to develop the hide of a rhinoceros, whereupon they all erupted into laughter, much to my surprise. What in fact I had said was that I had developed the hind of a rhinoceros, which friends assured me could have been equally applicable.

Giving talks can be quite cathartic. If you ignore the three weeks leading up to the event, where you experience increasing degrees of terror at the thought, they can be a wonderful opportunity, whilst you have a captive audience trapped in a room with you, to vent and air all your frustrations and gripes. Normally when I go off on one people just wander off.

*   *   *

If you haven't already glazed over by now, and while I'm on a roll, I really would like to tell you about one of my favourite bones of contention ……. MONEY.

As you know, when I went into this business I was not exactly a fledgling, and was sort of aware that being an artist might not be the most lucrative of jobs. But at that time I was ok ish in terms of having enough money to live on and even for little extra treats like day trips and new shoes, so I admit I was probably looking at my new future with fairly optimistic and misguided eyes. Anyway, as I have said, the 'thing' had grabbed me and wasn't going to let go, so I surged forwards into what I naively imagined to be the innocuous waters of the art world, without being aware of the scavengers lurking under the surface, waiting to gobble up my ideals and profits. I had certainly not realized just how severely my dedication to my new career would be put to the test in terms of just surviving as an artist.

I have always, apart from a few years when I was a 'kept woman' had to support myself financially, as of course do millions of artists, in a profession which is notoriously precarious when it comes to making a living. It is the only job I can think of (writers included) where it's not so much a question of when you are likely to be paid, but more one of if. BUT, and let me make this quite plain, I AM NOT COMPLAINING ABOUT THIS FACT, no, absolutely not. I went into the art world with my eyes at least partially open. No-one made me choose the path I am on, and I have always been fully accepting of the nature of what I do being a 'dodgy' business in monetary terms.

I am completely understanding of the fact that art or rather the buying of art is a luxury business that people can do without, unlike their holidays, washing machines and state-of-the-art designer kitchens, and of course you can't make anyone like a painting, let alone want to buy one…. try though you might. No-one made me become an artist, I walked towards it of my own free will.

No, the reason I am moaning yet again is nothing to do with all that. It is however to do with a very common attitude that seems to be prevalent among the non-artist fraternity regarding the worth and pricing level of a painting.

Let me start off by making an analogy. Imagine this scenario:

'Joe has just left school, or university, whichever you prefer, and has just landed a job working for a large company. As Joe has no experience within that firm, he starts off as the office junior (or dogsbody person, or whatever they are called these days), and his salary of course reflects the level he is at.

He is bright and hardworking, and gradually, over the years, he works his way up through the ranks, whilst his salary has been rising steadily too. Now Joe is on the management. He's not the Managing Director, yet, but he has nevertheless achieved quite a lot and understandably he is now receiving a salary that reflects this. I don't think anyone would argue that this isn't fair'.

SO WHY ISN'T IT THE SAME FOR ME?

During the thirty years I have been a painter, I have gained respect in my field, I exhibit in some good, established galleries, and I've won several prizes in some prestigious art competitions. But despite all this, lots of people (themselves often in well paid jobs), feel that an artist shouldn't price their work according to their skill, experience and worth.

Many people don't realise that the price of a painting you see on a gallery wall, is NOT the amount that the artist actually gets. Most professional galleries take between 45-50% commission, in London this is sometimes more. I am with a gallery now that is sympathetic to artists and takes a slightly lower commission – but his is unusual. A gallery of course has it's overheads and is promoting you and providing a showcase for your work. If an artist is serious about their career and wishes to make a name for themselves, they will need their work to be seen by as wide an audience as possible, which will not be achieved from their spare room at home. A large proportion of the artist's customers are provided by the gallery's client list and passing trade, and most galleries will print out invitations and lay on a private view if you are having a show with them, so we do need galleries. The proportion that a gallery takes could arguably said to be unfairly high, remember they have lots of artists on their books, whereas there is only one of me, but I don't want to shoot myself in the foot here, so I'll give gallery owners the benefit of the doubt and spare them, along with Aunty Minnie, from the firing squad should the Revolution come about. No, hang on, second thoughts, I just won't put them too near the top of the line-up.

Out of the approximate half of the asking price of a painting that I receive, I have to buy my materials (not cheap and constantly having to be replenished); pay for my framing (also not cheap); run a car (even more expensive, but I need to be able to get my work around to galleries and get to workshops etc.); pay my rent (this is actually quite reasonable as I have a sympathetic landlord at the moment; pay tax, if I have actually earned anything that year (it's the only time I am happy to make a healthy loss); pay my rates and bills etc..... want me to go on? Oh, yes I nearly forgot, eat. Yes, funnily enough, artists are just like everyone else, they need to eat too.

So you will start to see that actually, I don't take too kindly to hearing civilians saying things like "huh, they're a bit expensive aren't they"; "heck, look at the price of that"; and "oh I wouldn't pay that for a painting, it doesn't look like it's taken very long does it".

I've even been knobbled by a few gallery owners at odd times regarding the pricing of pictures, during economic climate changes. Let's face it, a gallery would rather get a percentage of ten pence, than nothing, but if I were to reduce my prices what would I get ….. not even enough to cover the parking fee on a gallery visit, and I don't seem to remember any mention of reduction in gallery commission when 'times is 'ard'.

The predicament I have is such that if I sold a painting to someone last year for a certain price, that customer doesn't want to see a similar painting by me a year later selling for a lower price than they had paid for their piece. It just isn't professional to go backwards. Customers want to feel that they have invested in something that is going up in value, not down, so I have to more or less stay true to my pricing level and hope that things will pick up.

In reality, my prices haven't gone up at all for quite a long period of time, unlike the cost of living, so next time someone on a nice fat regular salary implies that a painting is too expensive, I'm wondering if I would be justified in breaking their nose.

I have heard many crass comments regarding this issue, over the years, not always about my own work (although I've had my fair share), but often about other artists work too. They are usually made by those civilians that have little or no knowledge about art.

I think more than probably this sort of attitude stems from the fact that people often find it hard to differentiate between painting being a hobby and it being a profession, but also from an archaic stereotypical tradition that we should expect artists to be struggling. It has become a tradition which is hard to shake. The unpredictability of whether or not you will actually sell a painting is bad enough, let alone having to try to justify asking a fair price when you do. Admittedly, once an artist has 'hit the big time', it could be argued that there are instances where their pricing level can become somewhat inflated, in the same way that professional footballers can command disproportionate salaries. In saying this, perhaps I am doing the very thing I am accusing civilians of and no doubt if ever I reached those dizzy heights I would find a way of justifying my ill gotten gains.

As a professional painter that is fully aware of the nature of the world I am in, I have no problem with anyone coming up to me and saying "I really like your work Wendy, but I'm afraid I can't afford to buy a piece at the moment". I do however have a problem with someone that knows nothing about me or about painting, saying "your work is too expensive". How do they know?

I have on occasions heard someone say "oh, a painting is only worth what someone will pay for it". What rot! A painting is worth what it is worth, not what some chancer that comes along says they are prepared to give you for it. That would be like me going into a travel agent and saying "I'd like to book that holiday in Italy for two weeks, but I've only got fifty quid, so that's what it's worth and that's what I'll pay for it.

*   *   *

Another very common misconception is to do with time. I defy any artist in the world to argue with the fact that the most commonly asked question that they will receive throughout their time on earth will be "HOW LONG DID IT TAKE"? My own personal answer to this question is "thirty bloody years". When you are discussing a painting with someone, this is the one thing that will be guaranteed to pop up.

People will often equate the worth of a painting with how long it has literally taken the artist to do. In fact, it has little to do with that, but much more to do with the journey the artist has had in getting to the point where they can do that piece of work, and ultimately of course in whether that picture is successful or not and is visually pleasing to the eye, irrespective of journeys or hours and minutes.

What you see on the wall reflects the confidence, knowledge and experience that I have gained during the time I have spent tearing my hair out over the years I have been working as an artist. The finished painting is the icing on the cake.

If you are still insisting on me justifying my credibility as an artist by equating it with how I spend my time, you'll be pleased to know that I do in fact spend a considerable amount on what I think of as my 'build-up' period.

At this preparatory stage, which incidentally can take weeks, or even months, I would usually be thinking about working on a batch (I wonder what the collective word for several paintings might be, perhaps a palette or a splat or something). Anyway, it would comprise me going out photographing, sketching, sawing-up and priming huge lumps of board, planning out and designing compositions on small roughs, over and over again, until I have refined them to the point where I feel satisfied, then drawing up the finished designs onto the prepared boards, ready to start painting. These early processes are essential for me, not least because they enable me to stave off the terrifying moment when I must face the music and squeeze out some paint.

When I can't avoid it any longer, I choose to do the surface painting quite quickly because I like the type of painting which is energetic and shows energy and emotion (and believe me there is plenty of that going on) in the mark-making, and I enjoy the potential for serendipity that this brings with it. There is something exciting and a bit terrifying about working with a medium like oil paint, which is not only unstable in it's composition, but has the ability to dribble and run. It can feel a bit like trying to manipulate and control jelly.

So, to take stock, we've established that we are dealing with not only a flaky artist here, but also an unstable medium. It's not boding well is it?

Now this is where you sign on the dotted line for the life-long subscription to 'let's be nice to the artist' magazine. I am appealing to all you civilians out there, that's those of you that are blessed with sane and happy lives, to show some compassion and even just a little bit of understanding to those of us that are doomed to a life of turmoil and instability, and well, to handle us with care.

Just remember that as creative people, we need to have our thoughts and feelings near the surface, so that we can pop them into our work at the drop of a beret, without having to haul them up from our knees every time we feel the urge to express ourselves coming on. (Please try not to misinterpret what I have just said).

Everyone is familiar with the old cliché about the artist having an 'artistic temperament', well sod it, I don't care if I am lynched for saying it, yes, I think there may be some truth in this. Just imagine all that creative energy and emotion bubbling away under the surface, a bit like Vesuvius waiting to erupt, no wonder we might appear to be a bit touchy or over sensitive on occasions.

*   *   *

I do hope by this time, that I am beginning to woo you over a little. In fact the purpose of me going on like this, is to give you civilians half a chance in trying to understand your artistic friends. Oh, you don't have any; no? you don't want any either, very wise, and to give you some guidance in 'handling' we sensitive souls. You see I am trying to help you.

On no, it's no use .... I'm trying to be reasonable, but I'm sorry, I just can't keep it up. Look, I've shown that I can be quite magnanimous. I've acknowledged and praised those dear civilians that are sweetie-pies, but I do still feel that it is my duty to turn the tables once again and to warn any would-be artists about the hazards of what to expect from a big chunk of the general populous.

CIVILIANS ARE LURKING EVERYWHERE. They are in the guise of your husbands and wives, that nice woman down the road in the corner shop, the TV repair man, your best friend, and even your sweet little bed-ridden mother ...... and they are waiting to crush you with their casual, thoughtless criticisms : "But darling, you've missed out the telegraph pole that's outside that cottage"; "Why have you done the trees that funny colour"; "I don't think you've quite got his nose right" (well you try spending four hours trying to get the bloody thing to look like it belongs on someone's face); "How much are you paying for those art classes"?

 The fact is, dear friends, it is easy to criticise something which you know nothing about, but please spare a thought for the 'beginner' that is struggling to master one of the confusing amount of mediums there are to choose from; watercolours, oils, gouache, acrylics, egg tempera, pastels, charcoal, ink etc. etc., the list is endless. The one thing that they all have in common? ...... they are all bloody hard to get to grips with. Then once your friend has decided on which one to go for and splashed out on the correct paper and an equally bewildering variety of brushes (most of which they will never use), they then find themselves in the tricky position of trying to make their subject matter look like something remotely recognisable.

 After a year or so of this they will spend the remainder of their time as artists trying desperately to undo all that and attempting to put their interpretation of what they see down, instead of simply copying what's in front of them. It sounds bonkers even to me, and that is precisely what I have been attempting to do over the last thirty years, but sadly it is the curse of the artist to feel a need to do this.

Oh why can't we just make do with the world the way it is. Why must I paint the fields red and the cows blue, why oh why? But there we have it. Matisse saw his world in terms of colour, shape and pattern, Picasso became hell bent on making his models all look like they needed cosmetic surgery and Monet went through life convincing himself that the world is really a lovely hazy, muzzy mass of little fragments of colour; of course we can't rule out the fact that this may have had something to do with the fact that he had terrible eyesight so he was probably just painting what he could see.

Isn't it interesting, what a load of lemmings we are. The fact that one poor bloke that needed his cataracts sorting could head up a whole art movement, is testament to the need for artists to have some kind of trend to follow.

The more I think about it, the more I am beginning to see that artists must be quite an arrogant lot. Who exactly do we think we are? What, are we so important that we can't just make do with the world as it was Created? I can begin to see that you civilians might have a problem in understanding and sympathising with our megalomaniacal tendencies. Yet all I'm asking for is a tiny bit of compassion and tolerance, in allowing us our place, alongside you lucky, untroubled folk, you who are prepared to just accept that the grass is green, without trying to change it all the bloody time.

But you know, we are quite harmless. If it helps, think

of us as being a bit ill or just plain nutty. Don't we deserve your sympathy?

*   *   *

I must say that offloading all this is proving to be extremely cathartic (although I'm not sure what it's doing for you). If I was an American I'd be saving a fortune on therapists' fees. Anyway, I am sorry for all the moaning, but in fact, I haven't quite finished yet...... ho ho no, not by a long shot.

People go into art for all kinds of reasons; some join art societies or attend evening classes; some prefer to do it at home; and some, like myself, want to go the whole hog and have given themselves up to a life sentence.

Many people are keen to improve their skills, and some enjoy attending classes simply because they are interested in Art, or that they enjoy the social aspect of mixing with like-minded people. The lovely thing about Art, is that it is a huge umbrella under which we can all crouch, quite happily alongside each other, for whatever reason we may have of being there. There is though, a small proportion of people that have entered the Art world by sneaking in through the back door, which brings me on to another one of my favourite gripes that I want to share with you, that is my aversion to the POP-UP ARTIST.

You'll already be familiar with pop-up shops, pop-up exhibitions, and even trendy pop-up galleries, that have a tendency to spring up in disused gas showrooms and such places, nothing wrong, as far as I can see, with any of those. The pop-up painter however, takes the biscuit when it comes to sheer, bare-faced cheek.

First of all, let me make it absolutely clear, I am NOT referring to any determined, would-be artists that have flair or talent, whether they have been doing art as a hobby, are self-taught, or are new to the art world, either because they are young and just starting out, or because they have not previously had the opportunity to pursue their interest in practicing art. I know of several students, young and old, that are hardworking, talented and serious about what they do, and they deserve to have an opportunity to show their work in any notable gallery. No, I am referring to the breed of people (I can't bring myself to call them artists), who don't posses any of the above, but do have massive quantities of delusional arrogance and cheek.

These are often people that have cushioned lives, and think it would be fun and rather interesting to get up one morning and attach a label to themselves that reads 'artist'. I say these people are delusional, because despite having an innate inability to draw or paint, and despite the fact that they have up until that time, shown little interest in art, let alone having ever had a go themselves, are determined to push in, attempt to jump on an existing artist's bandwagon and expect the same artist to 'open doors' for them.

They push themselves forward at previews and demand introductions. They are people that get up one morning and decide that it would be nice to be an artist for a change, and well, after all, any monkey can do art, can't they. Today I'm a bank manager/deep sea diver/plumber/actor/comedian – tomorrow a painter – just like that. I could name at least one very well-known celebrity, whose pretentious splatterings I spotted in a gallery, along with the accompanying bullshit describing his 'art', who falls into the 'I'm already famous, so let's use that fact to launch myself into an additional career as an artist' category. I had a strong suspicion at the time, when I saw his exhibits, that when he had approached the venture, he'd had more than a little of his tongue thrust into his cheek, but that just made me even madder. How would he like it if I'd gone up to him when he was performing and said "go on shove over, let's have a go, I could do what your doing".

I was at an arty social do quite recently. After chatting to a woman for a while, I asked her if she was an artist. She replied "oh, I haven't decided yet, but I have done a couple of sketches". There have not been many occasions in my life in recent years, where I have been rendered speechless.

But hey, what a lovely idea; it's a bit like playing Dr's and nurses as a child isn't it. Wouldn't it be great if we could just get up in the morning and decide to be whatever we wanted, overnight. Now, let's see, what do I fancy ...... I know, I think I'll be a geologist today. Oh come on, how hard can it be to dig up a few stones ..... now, where did I leave that garden trowel. Oh I don't know though, I quite fancy having a go at dentistry, "go on mate, give us a go on your molars".

Blimey, the world's my oyster, if only I could just get rid of this nervous twitch that I've developed.

Oh ho ho, I am aware of the irony in me writing this. 'Today I'm a painter, tomorrow a writer', but in my defence, at least I know what I'm writing about.

The pop-up artists are very often people that have the wherewithal to network in the 'right crowds', to talk-the-talk, and impress their audience with who they know.

Yes, I am annoyed that these people get good opportunities to exhibit in notable galleries, whose owners are prepared to sell their critical judgement down the pan in order to have the movers and shakers on board, irrespective of the banality of their work.

The pop-ups will spend an entire preview of someone else's work, wittering on tirelessly about their own efforts and plans for the future, without making even a passing comment about the work on show. They will barge in if they see you talking to anyone who they think might be useful to them, practically knocking you out of the way. They have PhD's in networking.

I once went out with someone who fancied himself as a part-time 'professional' artist. He already had a really well-paid job in finance and had splashed out on the sort of art equipment that would have graced the shelves of any leading art retailer's premises. He obviously liked art, which was great, and I was pleased that he had the inclination to actually take up painting himself ...... as a beginner .... or so I thought. But no, silly me, I had not realised at this point, that he had in fact arrived, and that he was so clever that he could just dismiss going through the preliminaries of actually learning anything about painting or drawing. This chap had spent five days on a landscape painting holiday in France, had attended a two-hour talk on portrait painting at the local library, and to date had produced four pieces of very dubious quality work plus a few quick sketches.

You can imagine how flabbergasted I was one evening over dinner, when after briefly mentioning a forthcoming exhibition that I had coming up, he started talking about the practicalities of him getting an opening in some of Wales's leading art galleries. Initially I thought he must be joking and I laughed, until I saw the annoyed expression on his self-satisfied chops. How marvellous it must be though, to have that much belief in yourself.

Now I am not an ungenerous person and have always tried to give as much as I am able to in terms of passing on knowledge, or even the odd leg-up if I have ever been in the position to do so, but more importantly, if the recipient has 'earned their stripes'. It isn't even that I want everyone else to suffer for their art and get there through toil and anguish (oh alright, perhaps just a tad), but I do honestly feel that to get to the stage where you can call yourself a professional anything, you do at least need to have acquired a tinsy bit of experience in that field.

The problem is, that unless you've tried it, art, or painting, is often seen as a soft option. My hairdresser has said that this attitude is also prevalent in her profession.

I can recognise the worth and necessity of other jobs; we need banks and solicitors, and we need mechanics and plumbers. But we also need painters, writers and musicians to feed our souls. All I'm asking is that artists are treated with the same consideration as other professionals, and not as brainless airheads, that are not in a serious profession and that only deserve respect once they have 'made it'.

Oh I know you could argue that what I do, doesn't save lives, or alter the axis of the planet, but wouldn't our lives be a bit dull, a bit black and white, without the soul searching offerings of the artist.

Think about the enormity of the role of artists; think about what they provide in the society in which we live. Look around the room you are in at this very moment (hopefully not the toilet); every single thing in that room has been designed, from the house itself, to the pattern on the curtains; the chair you are sitting on and the pictures that adorn your walls, to the pen you are using to write to the Times, your letter of complaint about what I have written here. Textile designers; product designers; furniture makers, ceramicists; fine art painters; weavers; photographers; wood turners; sculptors, graphic designers and the stack of authors and poets whose works are stuffed into your bookcase …… oh, and perhaps you are listening some nice music that has been created by someone…… and what is the thing all these people have in common? ……. Oh yes, they are Artists and Designers; they have all created something that will embellish our lives, whether it be on a decorative or a functional level.

Art comes in all shapes and sizes, but we are all enriched by it.

*   *   *

Judging from some of the comments I have heard over the years from people, we are often perceived to be hedonistic layabouts leading decadent lifestyles and sipping absinth all day in our dressing-gowns. Personally

I'd rather have a latte and a chocolate digestive.

What people often don't realise, when they think of us dabbling away in our garrets with our smocks on, is that being an artist is not a 9-5 job. When 'normal people' are tucked up in their armchairs or beds, many artists are beavering away into the small hours. The belief that artists don't really work, is far from reality, in truth, artists more often than not work longer, more unsociable hours than the average civilian.

Artists might not break the law, but they can often break the social rules in terms of conventionality. Being a fully paid-up member of the art world means that you are often deemed to be classless (which is not a bad thing), slightly out on a limb and slightly on the edge. The fact that we don't conform to any standard group, renders us oddities, to be viewed with puzzlement and even amusement. But we are not seen as any threat to more conventional or 'normal' members of society, so try to think of us with tolerance rather than as misfits that don't deserve the same living standards as other people.

I suppose the somewhat archaic attitude towards artists by civilians is partly our own fault, because in truth, we haven't really moved on that much from the time of the cave dwellers. Other jobs have got quicker with technological progress, and although artists have more choice and freedom to express themselves now, and although we may have moved on from the Cistine chapel to Marcel Duchamp's cistern, when it comes to drawing and painting, well, that still takes us the same amount of time as it did in Neanderthal times. There we all are, still just scratching away on a surface. If I am teaching a group of students for the first time, I always tell them not to worry if it goes wrong, because at the end of the day, a drawing is just a load of dirty marks on a piece of paper.

If anything, attitudes towards users of the right side of the brain have regressed in some ways. Gone are the days when you were considered to be in a respected profession if you were an artist, now-days it is more common to believe that artists are artists because ..... well .... there not much cop at anything else are they, so are unable to go out and get a 'proper job'. But you can bet on your granny's life, as soon as you have 'made it' you will join the ranks of 'the respectable' again.

Not so very long ago, in lots of rural parts of Wales and England, if an artist was seen to be depicting scenes from nature, unless you were making decorative patterns, which were allowed, you would be considered to be a sinner, flying in the face of God; that was His work, so you would be seen as making 'craven images'.

It is interesting that the attitude towards artists abroad is that on the whole, the continentals embrace art and artists as a valued part of everyday life. While Mihangel was being ostracised by his nearest and dearest here on home turf, he spent some time walking and drawing his way around Spain and Italy, where he was taken home and fed and generally treated like a king.

In Ireland artists are exempt from paying tax, because it is recognised that they are in an impossibly precarious profession as regards earning a living.

Let me leave you with another quote that an artist friend received some years ago from a couple who had acquired a painting from my pal. He had trustingly but foolishly, because he knew the people, allowed them to take the painting and let them pay in installments, despite the fact that they were very well-heeled. As they now had the painting on their wall at home but were proving to be very slow in coughing up, he tentatively and politely suggested it might be time to pay for the piece, as he was literally starving at the time. Bear in mind, he was painfully thin, looked ill, and his hair was falling out. Their reply was "oh come on, you can wait a bit longer, everyone knows that artists need to suffer in order to produce meaningful and profound work".

FEEDING MY HABIT

Wendy Murphy

The extent of my inheritance runs to my father's calves, a £100 premium bond, and a silver icing sugar spoon, so I realised a very long time ago that given the nature of the business I am in, I would have to do all sorts of other work in order to feed my habit of being a painter. As I have said, I am fully accepting of this fact, and on the whole, apart from the times when I lapse into self-pity, I go to my various jobs with, well perhaps cheerfulness is not quite the right word, but at least with a quiet forbearance of martyrdom. In fact, if you see me with my hand down someone else's toilet, and I look like I'm smiling, don't be fooled, I've probably just got a touch of wind.

Anyway, the fact is that over the years, I have done many part-time jobs that have enabled me to carry on painting. The part-time teaching is undoubtedly the most demanding, frustrating and fulfilling of these jobs. It has done wonders for my confidence and I have, during this time, met some lovely people. Despite the difficulties that dealing with people in a creative context, no let's be honest, people in general, can throw up, I have often felt fond of my students (both young and old); my empathy for these people comes I believe, from the fact that as a practicing artist, I am fully aware of the hell they are going through.

As you may imagine, living in a rural area means that part-time jobs are not exactly in abundance, in either variety or quantity, so during the Summer months, and when 'times is particularly 'ard', I put on my designer pinny (one has one's appearances to keep up) and arm in arm with Mr Muscle I go off in pursuit of various cleaning jobs.

Because holiday changeovers often fall on the same day, I have on occasions been in the uncomfortable position where I find myself double-booked and then have the frantic task of doing a five hour cleaning job in two and a half hours in order to fit both jobs in before the guests arrive (invariably at least an hour before they are officially meant to). There are times when I have had four or even five cleaning jobs on the go, but as I am continually reminded that one has to suffer for one's art, I can only imagine that this is good for me.

It's my hands I feel most sorry for. Visiting a ninety-six year old in a nursing home recently, I noticed with a shock that my hands looked older than hers.

I had a wonderful job a few years ago though, working in a high-class gallery/gift shop, which was a forty minute drive from where I live. I vaguely knew the owner, through a mutual friend that worked there, and was flattered one day when she asked me if I would like to become her 'Saturday girl'; oh alright Saturday person then, if you're going to nit-pick.

This was a place that I had spent many a wasteful, but happy hour in, drooling over the lovely things, so the thought of spending days at a time there, with 20% off the goodies, was too much. I explained sadly though, that owing to the fact of me being numerically challenged, it would be impossible for me to take the job on, particularly as they had an old-fashioned till that didn't work out the change for idiots like me. She poo-poo'd my fears and insisted that I would be wonderful for the job, (ha ha, little did she know).

A kindly friend said that she would 'play shops' with me, a few days prior to the dreaded first day. After five minutes, she looked troubled and said "oh, you are quite bad aren't you".

Even now after several years, as I write this, I can feel my palms sweating as I remember the terror I felt, standing behind the counter on that first morning ….. no, lets be honest, for the next six months, praying to God that no-one would buy anything. My heart would lurch with fear every time someone entered the shop.

Those early customers would take pity on me when I explained that I was new and not yet used to shop work (I was still using this excuse a year later). They would tentatively suggest what change I needed to give them, whereupon I would thrust my hand into the till and dutifully cough-up. Any one of them could have been chancers and taken advantage of the situation, but as the business was still solvent at the end of the year, they were obviously decent folk.

As I began to relax, I grew to love that job. I would never be great at the money side of things, but discovered I could cope, providing nobody upset the apple-cart by offering to give me the odd ten pence or whatever they thought would be a help to round off the amount, so that I could give them less small change, or for whatever purpose it is that this serves. You see, I still don't understand what I'm talking about now, when it comes to this sort of thing.

Anyway, I loved chatting to the customers, and I loved getting a bit dressed up to go to work; it made a change from standing in my garret in paint smeared overalls and stinking of turps. My fingernails were a bit of a problem though, because no matter how hard I scrubbed, it was impossible to destroy the evidence of my latest romance with Prussian blue, and no matter how many airs and graces I tried to put on, and no matter how hard I tried to pretend that I was in fact the owner of the place, my hard work was always undone as soon as the customer glimpsed my yucky hands. I have had a similar response in supermarkets, but as I can't be bothered to put nail varnish on and to keep touching it up, I have to accept that people just think I'm dirty.

The thing that I loved most of all about working at this establishment was being surrounded by all the gorgeous stuff. I don't believe I ever actually took much money home, because I would invariably take advantage of my 20% staff discount and convince myself that I really couldn't do without whichever of the lovely pieces of jewellery/cards/bags/ceramics that happened to take my fancy at that particular time.

My boss was so concerned for my welfare in the end, that I was banned from buying anything. We would have big arguments in front of the customers, where she would stand hissing at me that I should try to see the error of my ways, and I would argue the point that I really would find it impossible to do without the green earrings that were exactly the same colour as my new jumper that I had felt forced to buy because it was this season's colour, according to Cosmopolitan which I had needed to get in order to fill the time on the train journey I'd had whilst visiting that new TK-Max in Shrewsbury, you know, the one with all the designer second's. Well God damnit, I'm only human!

Now, I might not be too bright when it comes to adding up, but you've more than probably worked out by now that I have a Professorship when it comes to spending money. I liken myself to a tree or plant that pushes up it's most spectacular blooms, aware that it's death is imminent, as I rush out and frantically spend my last few quid, knowing it is only a matter of days before the letter from the bank hits the mat.

The owners of the gallery are both painters, so apart from all the other goodies they stocked, they had their own paintings adorning the walls too.

I learnt that the trick in trying to sell a painting is in reverse psychology. Too keen and you'll have the punters running. Act like you don't give a shit, (lets face it, if it's not your own work, the chances are you won't) and you've got them where you want 'em. Locking the door should only be used as a last resort, when they say they're just popping down the road for a coffee while they decide which one of the two pictures that they have been agonizing over for the past three hours, (on the wall, off the wall, by the window, on another wall, by the window again), they will go for. By this time you know the layout of their house as if you'd designed it yourself. Only then do you lock the door, because you have learnt that once they step outside you will never see them again.

Then there are the customers who can't bring themselves to leave the premises without making excuses and feeling terribly embarrassed or guilty if they haven't bought anything; "If only the colours were a bit more muted"; "If only it was a centimetre bigger"; "If only there was a small square of red in the top left hand corner"; If only it was a completely different bloody picture and they hadn't just spent-up in the rival gallery down the road. If only they would just admit that they think its all shite and wouldn't have any of it on their walls in a million years.

Of course art appreciation is subjective, and everyone is entitled to their tastes and opinions (just as long as they choose mine).

I did for a time, think that working there might prove

to be a good opportunity to meet someone interesting that might 'take me away from all this', after all I was wearing my best clothes. I suppose I saw it as a sort of retail dating agency. Unfortunately, the only blokes that seemed remotely interesting tended to have a nice little wife in tow and would sickeningly be treating her to that gorgeous necklace that I'd been drooling over for the last two months.

Anyway, it all came to a head one day when my boss got wind of my flighty ways and sarcastically offered to put my 'details' up in the window. I had to accept that 'male-order' shopping was not going to work and sadly, I came to realise that the closest I was likely to get to 'fifty shades of grey', would be to do a tonal exercise with the students in college.

I finished up working at this establishment for eight years, before the owners couldn't take any more, either of me or the business, and retired. I have been much richer since they closed.

I have done a variety of odd jobs since I've been a painter, in order to not quite make ends meet. Whilst still a student in Canterbury I worked for an estate agent, where I would frequently double book clients for 'viewings', or forget to phone the owners back to warn them of impending visits, so that they would open the front door to find ten strangers standing on the step, and they hadn't even made the bed or put the budgie under the settee. Then of course there was that business with the photocopying machine.

I was sent to 'the outpost' in the end, where I was less likely to do any harm. This consisted of an unfinished show-home on a dreary new-build estate straight out of 'Lego-land, five miles out of town. I would spend the day reading, walking round the exercise yard like a prisoner, and generally lying through my teeth about the attractiveness of the houses to any prospective buyers that had stumbled upon the house and come in, in an attempt to shelter from the rain.

One particular such house that I had been seconded to hadn't even been finished to a degree where there were any door handles on the inside of the doors (or maybe this was a design feature), and I found myself one day in the unfortunate position of having to first of all politely call, then shout, and finally scream, from a tiny window, whilst standing on the toilet seat, to the site manager, who was in his little hut further down the estate, to come and rescue me.

I did have a cleaning job some years ago in a big posh hotel, where I would also be called in to wash-up on Saturday nights or when they were busy. It was during the time when 'nouvelle cuisine' was fashionable. You know the sort of thing, where guests would be given a large dinner plate, the outer rim of which had been wiped clean with a filthy old kitchen cloth last seen mopping up some residue from a raw chicken. On the plate would be a miniscule dollop of some kind of indistinguishable puree and something resembling a shoe horn sticking out of the top, served with a drizzle of what looked suspiciously like camel sick, but was in fact 'Rabbit's Ear jus'. But it was applied with an artistic flourish and did look quite pretty, which justified the fact that you had just spent a week's wages on it.

This job was a doddle, because there was never a speck of anything left on the plates, due more to the tiny portion than the quality of the food I fear. Dinner was usually served on plain white plates, after several guests were seen attempting to eat the pattern on more decorative ones and the local fish-n-chip shop flourished around this time, as famished punters would flock there immediately after their fine-dining experience. Not that I'm not sophisticated or anything.

Working at this establishment made me realise that I hadn't in fact been born into the wrong life, as I had suspected, when I was pulled up one day by the owner, for sweeping up the ash from the hearth, with that dear little brush which accompanies the crumb tray.

Yes, it was a sad moment when I acknowledged the fact that the closest I was ever likely to come to stepping out with Hooray Henry, would be to trudge along the carpets with his namesake. But it was alright, because I was still going to be a famous artist one day.

I would prefer not to talk about the job at the pizza parlour in Brighton which only lasted one night, and I didn't even turn up at the sausage-making factory as I didn't think I'd have the stomach for it.

*   *   *

Whilst I was still a student, during my time in Brighton, I had received a commission from a local taxi driver who wanted a portrait done of his wife. He came into the college one day with his request, and the secretaries of the Art Dept. either thought they would be doing me a favour or that they could have a laugh at my expense, but either way, I was given first option, and as it would be true to say that I would do almost anything for money, I accepted.

I nervously caught the train to my client's flat, which was a couple of stops outside Brighton, bearing my big state-of-the-arc, old-fashioned camera, so that I could get some reference material to work from.

The couple were very sweet and plied me with tea and cake, but I couldn't help noticing that they appeared to have been caught up in a sort of time-warp, as their living room looked straight out of a film set from the 1950's, complete with plastic flowers that used to come free with soap powder, a vinyl pouffe with a fluffy orange cover (or maybe that was more 60's), a formica table, and one of those ghastly clocks that have brass sun-rays radiating out from the face, which I have been indignantly informed are now considered to be 'retro' and incredibly sought after. The trouble is, when you are old enough to remember things like this the first time round and when your childhood home was filled with such treasures, it can be hard to look on them with fondness.

After about an hour, and just as I was beginning to feel like an extra from 'Call the Midwife', Rich disappeared into another room and after a couple of minutes returned, reverently clutching one of those pictures from Woolies that those of you that are old enough to remember, will know as 'The Dusky Maiden'. You know the type of thing; sultry black hair, shimmering skin, come to bed oriental eyes and an off the shoulder peasant blouse.

"This is Maria" he lovingly announced, "and we want you to paint Doreen here the same".

Perhaps I'd better explain at this point, that Doreen was small, dumpy and middle aged, with a mousy perm and glasses, and was wearing a white acrylic crew-necked jumper.

I also probably need to mention now, another little problem (to add to the list) that I have had since I was a child, that of laughing in completely inappropriate situations. The first time I realised my misplaced mirth was when a school chum informed me solemnly one day that her beloved hamster had died and I exploded uncontrollably into ill suppressed laughter. I remember my mother, suspecting me to have been inadvertently spawned from the devil, carting me off to the Dr's, in the vain hope that I could be cured, only to be told that it was a nervous condition and that I would have to live with it, along with my 'nervy tummy' and obsessive sock pulling.

All joking aside though, it's not funny when you find yourself in this painful situation. I once pushed a ring I was wearing so hard, that the stone popped out, in an attempt to control my sniggering when a friend whispered in my ear that the performers during a high-brow concert we were attending, looked like they had been stuffed, and had creaked as they walked onto the stage; it wasn't even that funny.

Anyway, where was I, ah yes back to Maria, or Doreen; I was trying desperately in my head, to morph these two lovely ladies into one. I mean, I know all about using 'artistic licence' and all that, but my creative imagination was being stretched to it's limits here.

I was going to have to take some photographs .....but no .... too late ..... the monster was growing inside me, taking hold and consuming every cell in my body; I could feel it welling up and beginning to escape, like an evil gas, through my nostrils, my eyes and my mouth; it was taking control of my muscles and nerve endings.

Meanwhile, Rich, Doreen and Maria were staring at me with puzzled expressions, as I covered my face with my hands and pretended to have a life-threatening choking fit. I am sweating as I remember how awful it was, as I had to keep pretending to cough and rummage in my bag and blow my nose in an attempt to hide my shaking shoulders.

It wouldn't have been so bad if they hadn't been so nice, offering to get me extra tissues and drinks etc. Even Maria looked down at me with a benevolent smile touching the corners of her luscious lips. I had thought about throwing myself into a mock-faint, in an attempt to escape the situation, but I couldn't keep still for long enough. I suppose the obvious thing would have been to have staged a 'fit', where I could have convulsed legitimately, but quite honestly I couldn't be bothered going through all that palaver with the ambulance etc. so I valiantly made the best of things and managed to click the shutter a few times and hoped I'd got some sort of recognisable images that I might be able to work from, before I made my excuses and fled.

When I collected my developed film from the chemist a week later, there was a printed slip in with the virtually unrecognisable photos which suggested that the subject had been moving when the pictures were taken.

I spent the best part of the next fortnight laughing over the other side of my face. Two bloody weeks, I wrestled with the pair of them ….. Maria, Doreen, Maria, Doria, Meeria, Meenaria, Dareeia, Mania, Dareene, Areenia, Mariareena, Diareena …… and so the monster 'Mareena' was born, just as I was reaching breaking point when I could take no more. I lived, wept, and slept my creation. I had fused two souls from opposite ends of the human spectrum, conjured up from memory; a hybrid that bore absolutely no resemblance to either of them. The mousy perm was now a warm fuzzy halo, framing shimmering, glowing cheeks where the smoker's lines had been magically hidden under a mask of Naples Yellow, Burnt Umber and Titanium White. The jumper had been cast off to reveal the sensual, sun-kissed shoulders that had lay dormant underneath.

When Rich came to the college for the 'unveiling', I felt so embarrassed that I decided not to charge him and simply own up to the fact that I hadn't managed to capture a likeness …… of either of them.

I nearly wept with incredulous relief when I saw through one eye that he was in fact delighted with the painting and wouldn't hear of my apologies (should have gone to Specsaves Rich); in fact he was so pleased that he gave me an extra twenty-five quid. I vowed never to darken the doors of portraiture again.

*   *   *

Of course, I'd be lying if I said I had remained true to my word. No, I am not a quitter. You've probably gathered by now that I have the tenacity of a leech, and a pretty stupid one at that. Even though I am aware that I am on a road to disaster I will keep going until I fall off, rather than give in and take the easy path by just giving up.

After the traumatic 'Mareena' episode, I found, a couple of years later, that my memory and flashbacks had dimmed enough for me to set off down the road of portraiture once again.

One of the many hair-brained money-spinning ideas I have had, was to do portraits of people. I was convinced this was my ticket to the sort of lavish lifestyle that I had not been born to.

I decided that rather than do them in oils, which would have taken longer and been less practical, I would do them in pastel. God knows what possessed me to choose this as the medium because the one thing that I absolutely hate using, in the whole world, is pastels. I loath the feel of them, I hate the smeary-ness of them, and I'm not keen on the fact that I feel like I've developed Emphysema after a stint of inhaling the dust they produce.

That was my first mistake. The second one was allowing myself to be coerced into offering 'freebies' to in the words of a friend, 'get the ball rolling'. I began to suspect my friend's motives, when this introductory stage, that had involved me doing pictures of her husband, children, house and dog, seemed to be going on for rather a long time, until in fact I finally had the temerity to suggest to my customers that they might like to give me a nominal contribution for my efforts, whereupon the orders promptly dried up.

The major flaw in this plan was that, apart from being dim enough to work for virtually nothing, I had already used up my quota of people (remember I live in a small community), so without splashing out an extortionate amount of money on advertising, which I didn't have, my source of potential clients was rapidly drying up.

If I'm honest, this was a relief in many ways, because I hated doing the bloody things. People would invariably give me a pitted, passport sized photo to work from, from which I would be expected to somehow get my rendering to look like it had hailed from planet earth.

I did one woman's entire family, which she was delighted with ..... until I got to the youngest granddaughter. Now bear in mind, I had never in my life met this girl and the photograph I had been given to work from looked like it had been stolen from 'The Borrowers' family album and dipped into a vat of acid, with the subject herself, wearing a rather attractive brace on her teeth, which I was instructed to leave off in the portrait.

I believe I worked a small miracle because I managed to make the girl look like a human being. I felt that I done particularly well in blessing her with a perfect set of gnashers, so Nana's spiteful comment that the picture wasn't bad, but I really hadn't got the mouth right, was particularly wounding.

Sorry, I've just had a little lie down. Anyway, I decided

I'd really had enough of people portraits, ….. but no, wait, hang on a minute …. there was still unexplored territory out there. Remember the leech.

If I were to say to you 'I am like a dog with a bone', this would provide you with quite a hefty clue as to where I'm heading next. Yep, you've got it …. PET PORTRAITS.

I decided to change my medium and do some, although I say so myself, rather fine pencil drawings, partly to give the lungs a rest.

My speciality was 'dead dogs', with the occasional pussy, and a few horses thrown in for good measure, although on the whole I tended to avoid anything equine, after a friend said that one of my gee gees looked like a pantomime horse.

Having gone through the awful sadness of losing my own beloved sheepdog at the age of seventeen (the dog I mean, not me), several years previously, I was very sensitive to the feelings of the owners of the deceased and only too aware of how important it was to try to capture 'our Charlie's' likeness. It's a great pity I wasn't working in watercolours during this time, because I would frequently sit weeping over the drawings, resulting in some interesting textures, especially in capturing a 'fur effect'.

I should think that you've more than probably got my measure by now, of what a kind and sensitive soul I am.

Unfortunately so did the punters, and I found myself falling victim to their pleas of "I'd dearly love a picture of little Piddles/Trixi/Fang to remember him by, but" ….. and here's the crunch ….. "I haven't got much money/I'm a pensioner/my husband's just dropped off his perch too, so if you do Pinky for half the price, I'll get you to do Ted as well".

There always seemed to be a reason for me not to get paid properly and it didn't take me long to realise that I was in fact, flogging a dead horse, and that this little venture, along with all the others was not going to provide me with my ticket to a better life.

*   *   *

Well meaning friends, have at various times, come up with the solution to my ongoing poverty by shoving a variety of possible beau's (what a lovely old fashioned word) my way, in the hope that I will be swept off my feet, and out from under theirs.

I can't begin to tell you of the unsuitability of some of these potential Romeos, but one of them actually ironed his newspapers before reading them. Darlings, I don't even iron my clothes, in fact I run a counseling service for people that do. I have not seen my iron for several years, but have a hazy recollection of strange clods of something being stuck on the bottom, after an adventure in paper-making.

I haven't totally given up on the idea of someone adopting me, but of course it's much harder to place older children isn't it.

As my friends haven't managed to palm me off onto anyone, and my sisters all have grandchildren, the task of looking after me falls to those unfortunate souls that are unlucky enough to live near by.

Having left my pride in the City, along with Christian Dior and any security, I spent the entire run-up to Christmas a couple of years ago, seeing how many times I could get myself invited out to dinner, culminating in the festive event itself being spent with my ex partner and his wife. Actually I spend every Christmas with them, (I like to keep a check on them, can't have them enjoying themselves too much can we).

My little dining out wheeze turned out not to be quite as bright a star as I'd imagined, in my quest to save a few bob, because by the time I'd forked out for wine and or chocolates for mine hosts and driven to their houses, I was worse off than if I'd stayed in and had egg and chips in front of the telly.

I seem to have brought a new dimension to the term 'care in the community'. I once heard someone say that artists are a bit like nuns – we need to provide, and take care of them. Yup! can't argue with that.

*   *   *

I was in such financial dire straights a couple of years ago, that I reluctantly decided to get an appointment to get some advice from my local 'we've got the answer to all your problems office'. After being advised to wait several months in order that I might see the person who was, I was assured, the best equipped to deal with my particular problem, i.e. being totally brassicered, I turned up for my appointment eventually, only to be told the chosen one hadn't come in that day, and was more than probably off having troubles of his own somewhere, (or possibly he had got wind of the fact that he would be dealing with me).

Either way, I was ushered into what appeared to be a grubby cupboard by the substitute advisor, who made a song and dance about obtaining every minute detail of my life since the age of 6 months.

As we progressed, I began to feel thoroughly cheered though, because this poor woman seemed to have more problems than me. The computer was playing up; she was in her words, 'in chaos and disorganised', having to take on her colleague's work load as well as her own; she had been forced to travel in that morning by bus, owing to the fact that her husband had had to take the car in because of the noise the engine had been making for the past two months, and how on earth was she going to get into town later to pick up her daughter's dry cleaning; she was still awaiting a knee op which would account for the way she struggled to make her way around the piles of whatever it was that were piled up in the cupboard; and finally I heard how, in her words again, she hated self-employed people like me, because we were so complicated to deal with, and this sort of thing really wasn't her bag anyway.

The general consensus, after several weary hours of her knocking things off the top of the piles, looking for information in the files on the piles, that she never seemed to find, shouting at me and the computer, was that the pitiful allowance that I might be entitled to, was not worth the bother, and if by some stroke of luck I had managed to sell anything along the way, I'd have to pay it all back at the end of the year anyway, thus putting me in the even more ghastly position of being in debt, on top of everything else.

Of course, she said accusingly "if you had six children you'd be laughing". Really?

The upshot of this merry morning was that after the initial furore of finding someone worse off than me, I came away feeling full of remorse for the trouble I had brought into her life, and a deep regret that I had not been more promiscuous during my fertile years.

I WISH I'D BEEN A BALLERINA

It's ok, take heart, there's a glimmer of light showing, we're nearly there.

During the years I have been a painter, my life has been, and continues to be rich, if not in monetary terms, certainly in colourful experiences, some of which have been wonderful, some not so great. But the one thing it has not been is dull.

I have frequently wondered if I am being tested, 'let's see how many difficulties she can handle; let's see if she's really serious about this art thing'.

I might not have managed many hurdles on the school playing fields, but believe me I've had to jump over a good few since. Yet despite all the problems, such as being permanently skint, and beating myself up over my work, I can say that at last, I have found a little corner of society where I fit. I can't begin to tell you how great it is to no longer be all alone, on the outside looking in, now that I've joined the ranks of 'weirdo's.

I've discovered that there are a whole load of us, ….. on the outside looking in ….. but together. I am proud to announce that I am one of the team now. Ok, it might not be the team, but at least it's a team.

If only I could have known as a child, that one day I would be united with my own tribe. I'd never have bothered with all that rubbish learning how to do forward rolls and stuff, which incidentally I am still waiting for an opportunity to put into practice. If only

I'd known, when I was hanging from the rafters, that there were other children out there, opting out of normal behaviour, training to become artists ..... but there we are, that's life I suppose.

There are times, when I wish I'd become a ballerina. At this stage in my life, I could have had a limp and been running a dance school for needy children and worn my hair in a bun, nice and tidy like. I would have attracted immediate sympathy from civilians, but more importantly, I would have known where I was, rather than feeling compelled to remain on this see-saw of unpredictability; 'can I get this damn painting that I've been wrestling with for the last two months to work; will I sell anything this month; will I sell anything next month; will I ever sell anything again; should I buy those sheepskin boots that I really need, or spend the money from the sale of that painting on replenishing my paints instead. I don't mind telling you, it's not easy being me.

Oh I know I may have been a wee bit hard on some of you civilians out there. Look, I'm sorry, alright. In truth, I have met some wonderful people that have been kind, supportive and understanding of the predicament I have often found myself in as a painter; all I'm really asking of those of you that are guilty of judging artists, is that you show us some tolerance, give us a bit of slack; make allowances for us over-sensitive souls and stop to think, before you make assumptions about us, or fall into the trap of repeating tired old clichés that stem back to medieval times.

I want to be shown the same respect that people who have careers in other fields are given, even if I am a bit of an oddball. Can't you just pretend that it's ok that we are all individual, 'Vive la difference' and all that, so that I don't have to be constantly reminded and made to feel like the 'weirdo' that I undoubtedly am. I'm quite harmless.

I don't want to live in a grey, even world, where we are all the same. I don't want to be a malteser, I want to take my equal place in the bag of pic-n-mix, and be treated the same as the big one with the purple wrapper.

Do just pause for a moment and think, might not Van Gogh, who incidentally only sold one painting in his entire lifetime, have managed to hang on to his full compliment of ears, if only he had not been so misunderstood and maligned by you lot.

It's too late for poor old Vincent, but it's not too late for you to change your ways. You could start by giving generously to the 'Artists' Benevolent Fund'. Please make your cheques payable to me and I will make sure your donations are put to good use; (where's the sheepskin catalogue)?

When it comes to having an open mind, of course everyone is entitled to their personal views about anything, Art included; but it might be worth remembering that this does include artists as well, so the next time you decide to say to anyone that will listen, that a piece of artwork is a load of rubbish, unless you have some experience of the subject or are an expert, it may be more prudent to stress that it isn't your cup of tea, but to at least acknowledge the fact that beauty is in the eye of the beholder.

*   *   *

I look at other people around me, with their pensions and retirement plans, and wonder what it feels like to get up in the morning, knowing that you have reached a point in your life when you can slow down and reap the rewards after a life of toil. But then I look at my own life and think how lucky I am to have discovered within me the thing that makes me tick, and to have had the opportunity to have a stab at it, to at least have a go at something that I find fulfilling, even if it's not always comfortable or rewarding.

I see my career as a painter very much in terms of a journey. It is a journey of development, which without wishing to immortalize myself, will never end, or rather it may only end on the day when the final thing I draw will be my last breath …. after that, well, who knows?

I will never be able to retire, because I'm like the sorcerer's apprentice, I can't stop. Painting isn't just my job, it's me. It isn't something that I can leave on the doorstep at 5 o'clock every evening, it's my whole identity. Even when I am not painting, I am never off duty. Not for me, the carefree trip to the seaside or the visit to the National Trust house, without the guilt of feeling that I should have brought my camera or sketchbook with me.

No matter how much I moan about it, and let's face it I do, I find that I've been swallowed up and like a Venus fly trap, it won't let me go. I have a compulsion to see it through to the bitter end. I wouldn't swap it for the world, but then I've always been a bit perverse.

Some years ago, when I had a friend staying and I happened to be going through …. let me see …… that would have been about my fifth mid-life crisis, (there have been seven to date), I announced in true 'drama queen' style "I'm going to give it all up", whereupon he wearily said "go on then".

I was furious!

Anyway, I can't give up, I've become addicted to turps.

Wendy Murphy

POSTSCRIPT

I'm a bit nervous that I might have shot myself in the foot here, so would just like to point out that of course I didn't mean all that stuff about galleries, workshops, punters and ballerinas (especially lame ones), and that you really shouldn't let it put you off buying my work or offering me a workshop (except still life), or even commissioning me to paint your dog. Oh, and that bit about the pop-up artists was very unfair, and …….

Oh, what the hell!

Wendy Murphy

ABOUT THE AUTHOR

Having tried unsuccessfully to escape, Wendy Murphy has finally given in after twenty-seven years and accepted that the corner of paradise where she lives in the North Wales village of Llwyngwril, is home. It is from here in her chilly garret, that she works as a professional painter, walks in the wild welsh hills and gazes out across Cardigan Bay.

She has won several prestigious awards for her painting, including having twice won the Laing Landscape Painting Competition for Britain; been runner-up in the Sunday Times Watercolour Competition and twice won the Welsh Open for MOMA Wales. With over twenty-six years teaching experience she is now devoting her time more fully to ~~shopping~~ painting.